Undergraduate Topics in Computer Science

T0214261

Undergraduate Topics in Computer Science (UTiCS) delivers high-quality instructional content for undergraduates studying in all areas of computing and information science. From core foundational and theoretical material to final-year topics and applications, UTiCS books take a fresh, concise, and modern approach and are ideal for self-study or for a one- or two-semester course. The texts are all authored by established experts in their fields, reviewed by an international advisory board, and contain numerous examples and problems. Many include fully worked solutions.

Also in this series

Iain D. Craig
Object-Oriented Programming Languages: Interpretation
978-1-84628-773-2

Max Bramer
Principles of Data Mining
978-1-84628-765-7

Hanne Riis Nielson and Flemming Nielson
Semantics with Applications: An Appetizer
978-1-84628-691-9

Michael Kifer and Scott A. Smolka

Introduction to Operating System Design and Implementation

The *OSP 2* Approach

 Springer

Michael Kifer, PhD
State University of New York
at Stony Brook, NY, USA

Scott A. Smolka, PhD
State University of New York
at Stony Brook, NY, USA

British Library Cataloguing in Publication Data
A catalogue record for this book is available from the British Library

Library of Congress Control Number: 2007926598

Undergraduate Topics in Computer Science ISSN 1863-7310
ISBN 978-1-84628-842-5   e-ISBN 978-1-84628-843-2

Printed on acid-free paper

Springer Science+Business Media
springer.com

Contents

Preface

$\mathcal{OSP}$ *2* is both an implementation of a modern operating system, and a flexible environment for generating implementation projects appropriate for an introductory course in operating system design. It is intended to complement the use of an introductory textbook on operating systems and contains enough projects for up to three semesters. These projects expose students to many essential features of operating systems, while at the same time isolating them from low-level machine-dependent concerns. Thus, even in one semester, students can learn about page replacement strategies in virtual memory management, cpu scheduling strategies, disk seek time optimization, and other issues in operating system design.

$\mathcal{OSP}$ *2* is written in the Java programming language and students program their $\mathcal{OSP}$ *2* projects in Java as well. Therefore as prerequisites for using $\mathcal{OSP}$ *2*, students are expected to have solid Java programming skills; be well-versed in object-oriented programming concepts such as classes, objects, methods, and inheritance; to have taken an undergraduate Computer Science course in data structures; and to have working knowledge of a Java programming environment, i.e., `javac`, `java`, text editing, etc. $\mathcal{OSP}$ *2* is the successor to the original $\mathcal{OSP}$ software, which was released in 1990 and programmed in C.

$\mathcal{OSP}$ *2* consists of a number of modules, each of which performs a basic operating systems service, such as device scheduling, cpu scheduling, interrupt handling, file management, memory management, process management, resource management, and interprocess communication. Projects can be organized in any desired order so as to progress in a manner consistent with the lecture material. The $\mathcal{OSP}$ *2* distribution comes with a reference Java implementation of each module, which is provided to the course instructor.

Each $\mathcal{OSP}$ *2* project has a well-defined API (application programming interface), that the student must implement in order to successfully complete the project. Thus, among other things, $\mathcal{OSP}$ 2 teaches students to work with "open" environments where programming must be conducted to satisfy concrete sets of project requirements and where APIs must be used to interface to other subsystems.

Each $\mathcal{OSP}$ 2 project consists of a "partial load module" of standard $\mathcal{OSP}$ 2 modules to which the students link their implementation of the assigned modules. The result is a new and complete operating system, partially implemented by the student. Additionally, each project includes one or more "*.java" files, which contain class and method headings for each of the assigned modules. These files serve as *templates* in which the student is to fill in the code for the required methods. This ensures a consistent interface to $\mathcal{OSP}$ 2 and eliminates much of the routine typing, both by the instructor and by the student.

The heart of $\mathcal{OSP}$ 2 is a simulator that gives the illusion of a computer system with a dynamically evolving collection of user processes to be multiprogrammed. All the other modules of $\mathcal{OSP}$ 2 are built to respond appropriately to the simulator-generated events that drive the operating system. The simulator "understands" its interaction with the other modules in that it can often detect an erroneous response by a module to a simulated event. In such cases, the simulator will gracefully terminate execution of the program by delivering a meaningful error message to the user, indicating where the error might be found. This facility serves both as a debugging tool for the student and as teaching tool for the instructor, as it ensures that student programs acceptable to the simulator are virtually bug-free. (Verification by the simulator does not, of course, replace the need to examine student programs to ensure that they are properly designed and acceptable from a software engineering point of view.)

The difficulty of the job streams generated by the simulator can be dynamically adjusted by manipulating the *simulation parameters*. This yields a simple and effective way of testing the quality of student programs. There are also facilities that allow students to debug their programs, including a detailed system log of events and various hooks into the system that allow student-provided methods to be called when an $\mathcal{OSP}$ 2 warning or error is detected. Also, a graphical user interface (GUI) is available that provides a convenient way for students and instructors to enter simulation parameters and to view various statistics concerning the execution of $\mathcal{OSP}$ 2.

The underlying model in $\mathcal{OSP}$ 2 is not a clone of any specific operating system. Rather it is an abstraction of the common features of several systems (although a bias towards Unix and the Mach operating systems can be seen, at times). Moreover, the $\mathcal{OSP}$ 2 modules were designed to hide a number of low-level concerns, yet still encompass the most salient aspects of their real-life counterparts in modern systems. Their implementation is well-suited as the project component of an introductory course in operating systems.

How to Use this Book

This book is primarily a manual for students on how to program the $\mathcal{OSP}\,2$ projects. Chapter 1 describes the overall organization of $\mathcal{OSP}\,2$. Chapter 2 takes the student through an example session with $\mathcal{OSP}\,2$. Each subsequent chapter constitutes a detailed description of one of the $\mathcal{OSP}\,2$ projects, beginning with a statement of the goals of the project, followed by a short introduction to the basic OS concepts relevant to that chapter's subject matter. The latter is intended to help bridge the gap between the $\mathcal{OSP}\,2$ manual and the course textbook. Before even the first assignment is handed out, students should read this Preface and Chapters 1 and 2. When a specific project is assigned (e.g. the thread-management project, project THREADS) the appropriate chapter (Chapter 4 in the case of THREADS) should be read carefully. Each project chapter provides a complete description of the API for the $\mathcal{OSP}\,2$ module the students have been asked to implement, including a clear account of the functionality of each method in the project. Also provided is a list of methods from other project modules that may be needed to implement the project assignment. The student should refer to the relevant chapters for a more detailed account of these methods.

Goals of this Book

Besides serving as the student project manual for $\mathcal{OSP}\,2$, the goals of this book, and more broadly the $\mathcal{OSP}\,2$ environment, are the following:

⋄ To teach students fundamental operating system concepts in the following areas:

  – process and thread management

  – memory management

  – file systems

  – interprocess communication

  – I/O device management

  – resource management

⋄ To give students the opportunity to practice these skills in a realistic operating systems programming environment.

⋄ To provide students with challenging individual and group programming assignments which promote "active learning" to reinforce and amplify the lecture material.

◇ To provide programming assignments that involve significant modifications to an actual, working operating system, thereby familiarizing students with the internals of OS implementation.

◇ To provide instructors with a flexible OS programming project that can easily accommodate their lecture schedule.

Acknowledgments

We would like to gratefully acknowledge the past members of the $\mathcal{OSP}$ $\mathcal{2}$ development team, including Sanford Barr, who produced the original design and implementation of the event engine; William Ries, Adam Sah and Tomek Retelewski, who, along with Sanford, designed and implemented an earlier version of $\mathcal{OSP}$ $\mathcal{2}$ that was written in C++; Fang Yang, who was responsible for porting the event engine and several other modules from the C++ version to Java; Kevin McDonnell and Peter Litskevitch, for designing, implementing and documenting most of the modules in the current version; Jingjing Wei, for implementing the latest configurable version of the GUI; Eric Nuzzi, who devised a systematic testing protocol for the $\mathcal{OSP}$ $\mathcal{2}$ code; Martin Bruggink, for implementing the PORTS module; Xiaohua Wu, for implementing the RESOURCES module; and David McManamon, for implementing the software that allows students to submit their solutions to $\mathcal{OSP}$ $\mathcal{2}$ assignments electronically.

Some parts of $\mathcal{OSP}$ $\mathcal{2}$ rely on third-party software. In particular, we thank Retrologic for developing their excellent Java obfuscator and releasing it under the Lesser Gnu Public License (LGPL).

Finally, we would like to thank Wayne Wheeler and Catherine Brett of Springer London Ltd for bringing their editorial expertise to bear on this project.

1
Organization of OSP 2

1.1 Chapter Objective

The objective of this chapter is to provide the essential general information about *OSP 2*, which is necessary in order to begin working with the system. This includes a description of the organization (breakdown into modules), instructions on how to compile, run and submit *OSP 2* projects, and general guidelines about programming *OSP 2*. Because of its introductory nature, this chapter should be read/reviewed before taking on any of the *OSP 2* projects your instructor may assign to you.

1.2 Operating System Basics

As explained in the Preface to this book, *OSP 2* is organized as a collection of modules, each corresponding to a class of resource that *OSP 2* is intended to manage. For your *OSP 2* programming assignments, your instructor will assign you one or more of these modules to implement, plug back into the rest of the system, and run via a simulation to ensure that your code is working correctly and efficiently. This chapter describes in some detail this division of *OSP 2* into modules and also provides you with other helpful information you will need to carry out your assignments. First, though, we shall step back and ask ourselves the questions: What is an operating system, and what kind of operating system is $\mathcal{OSP}$ 2?

What is an Operating System?   In order to understand exactly what $\mathcal{OSP}$ 2 is and how it is organized, it is useful to first consider the basic question: What is an operating system? Two generally held views are that an OS is an *extended machine*, and an OS is a *resource manager*. According to the first view, the function of an operating system is to present the user with the equivalent of an "extended machine" or "virtual machine" that is easier to program than the underlying hardware. This is accomplished through the operating system's *system call interface*: the collection of system calls that application programs may invoke to obtain one kind of service or another. For example, there are system calls to read and write files and to set the value of timers. Moreover, it is much easier to invoke these system calls to obtain system service as opposed to mucking around with hardware-specific instructions and machine registers, which one would be forced to do if there was no OS present.

Two well-known examples of system-call interfaces are the Win32 API (application programming interface) for various flavors of Microsoft Windows (Windows 2000/XP/Vista), and POSIX for the Unix flavor of operating systems, such as System V, BSD, and Linux. $\mathcal{OSP}$ 2 has its own system call interface, and you will be introduced to the system calls (Java methods) that constitute this interface in the subsequent chapters of this book.

According to the second view, an operating system is responsible for efficiently and fairly managing the resources of a computer system. These include processors (CPUs); memory (physical and virtual); devices such as disks; files and directories; and network connections (ports). By efficient, we mean that the OS should aim to maximize resource utilization whenever possible. By fair, we mean that users programs should be granted equitable allocation of resources during their execution. Note that most of the example resources we have listed are physical ones. One exception is files and directories. The part of the OS responsible for these "logical resources" is often called the file system.

As we will make clear later in this chapter, the view of an operating system as a resource manager is well suited to $\mathcal{OSP}$ 2, as $\mathcal{OSP}$ 2's system call interface is organized in terms of the various resources $\mathcal{OSP}$ 2 is intended to manage. More specifically, $\mathcal{OSP}$ 2 is organized into a number of modules—Java packages to be precise—and there is one such module for each type of resource $\mathcal{OSP}$ 2 is asked to manage. For example, there is an $\mathcal{OSP}$ 2 module for each of memory, devices, ports, etc., and each module exports (defines) a number of Java methods relevant to that module. Collectively, these methods make up $\mathcal{OSP}$ 2's system call interface.

Different Flavors of Operating Systems. To better understand $\mathcal{OSP}\,2$, it is also useful to realize that there are different flavors of operating systems available for the choosing. Some of those that immediately come to mind, and which you have probably heard of, are Unix, Linux, Windows, and MacOS. These systems differ mainly in the way they are structured and, of course, in their system call interfaces. Systems like Windows XP/Vista, Solaris (a version of Unix from SUN Microsystems), and Mach (an OS developed at Carnegie Mellon University in the 1980s and which later influenced a number of commercial operating systems, e.g., MacOS X) can be viewed as object-oriented in the following sense: basic system resources are represented as objects and there exist well-defined message-passing interfaces between objects.

Although $\mathcal{OSP}\,2$ is not modeled after any particular OS, a bias towards Unix and Mach can be seen in some parts of its architecture. The Unix bias is most evident in the FileSys package, where i-nodes are used to represent files stored on disk and directories map file names to i-numbers (inode indices). The Mach influence can be detected in the Ports package where Mach-like ports are used for interprocess communication. Mach also uses ports for exception handling (each process has an exception port), a topic not treated by $\mathcal{OSP}\,2$.

$\mathcal{OSP}\,2$ is an object-oriented operating system in the truest sense of the term. It is written in the object-oriented programming language Java. System resources and data structures are represented by classes, thereby providing well-defined method-call interfaces between objects à la Windows XP/Vista. And subclassing is used to specialize objects; for example, the I/O Request Block (IORB) is a subclass of Event so that threads can wait on it and be notified of its occurrence.

Another way in which operating systems differ, and which in some sense distinguishes older operating systems from newer ones, is whether or not they support *threads*. In older systems like Unix, executing programs are organized as processes: the OS is responsible for scheduling processes on the CPU and switching the CPU from one process to another for the purposes of *multiprogramming*. Multiprogramming is a technique aimed at increasing resource utilization. The basic idea is to have more than one process memory-resident at a time, and to switch the CPU from a process that has become blocked waiting for some event, say, the completion of an I/O operation, to a process that is ready to execute. In this way, the CPU is kept busy doing useful work most of the time, just the kind of thing a resource manager should strive for.

To conclude our brief look at multiprogramming, we should consider a little more carefully what it means to switch the CPU from one process to another, an operation commonly referred to as a *context switch*. Several steps are involved. First, the currently executing process must be removed from the CPU and placed on a queue associated with the event on which it is waiting. Then the process the OS has decided to schedule next for execution must be *dispatched* on to the CPU. This involves resetting a number of machine registers (such as the program counter, general-purpose registers, memory-management registers, etc.) to values associated with the newly dispatched process when it was last running. The execution of this process can now resume. This is an admittedly simplified view of what's behind a context switch; the subject is treated more thoroughly in Chapter 4.

In newer systems like Mac, Solaris, and Windows 2000/XP/Vista, the schedulable and dispatchable units of execution are no longer processes but rather threads; a process simply serves as a container for one or more threads. Processes of this kind are usually referred to as *tasks*, and that shall be the convention adopted in this book. So what does it mean for a task to be a "container" for threads? It means that the constituent threads of a task share the resources allocated to the task, including memory, files, and communication ports. As a result, switching the CPU from one thread to another is a lot simpler than switching the CPU from one process to another process as required in an OS that does not support threads. As we shall see, $\mathcal{OSP}$ 2 supports tasks and threads.

Operating Systems are Event-Driven.   Operating systems are a perfect example of so-called *event-driven* systems. As the name applies, an event-driven system goes into action in response to the occurrence of some event that it is familiar with. For example, a GUI (graphical user interface) program is an event-driven system that responds to clicks of the mouse made by the user; the precise piece of code that gets executed depends on what widget (tool-bar item, button, radio dial, etc.) gets clicked. In the case of operating systems, the events that an OS responds to include system calls made by user (or even system) programs, hardware interrupts, and machine errors. Event-driven systems are typically structured as one large case-statement contained in a while-loop that "catches" the various events the system is intended to respond to. When an event is caught, the case in the case-statement corresponding to that event is executed.

This kind of event-loop structure is indeed present in operating systems. Consider, for example, how a system call gets executed in a typical OS.The calling program first pushes the parameters of the system call on the system stack. The system call number is placed in a register and a trap instruction is executed to switch from user mode to kernel mode. The kernel examines the system call number and branches to the correct system call handler, usually via a table of pointers to system call handlers indexed on the system call number. At that point, the system call handler runs and, when finished, control may be returned to the calling procedure at the instruction following the trap instruction.

Hardware interrupts are handled in a similar event-driven way by an OS. In this case, a portion of system memory is set aside for the *interrupt vector*. Using the device number of the device that caused the interrupt, the interrupt vector may be indexed into to find the address of the interrupt handler for this device.

$\mathcal{OSP}$ *2* is also event-driven, not surprising given that, after all, it is an operating system. However, $\mathcal{OSP}$ *2* responds to *simulated* events. That is, at the core of $\mathcal{OSP}$ *2* is a simulator called the *event engine* (see Figure 1.1) that semi-randomly generates events of the kinds discussed above (system calls, hardware interrupts, etc.). In response to such an event, the appropriate Java method is called. For example, suppose the event engine generates an event corresponding to an instance of the system call for opening a file. Then the method **open()** in class FILESYS will be called. Moreover, if your instructor has assigned module FILESYS to you as a project, then it is the code that you wrote for method **open()** that will be executed in response to the event. This is actually a somewhat simplified view of how things work in $\mathcal{OSP}$ *2*. Section 1.9 explains $\mathcal{OSP}$ *2* event handling in greater detail.

What this all means is that in $\mathcal{OSP}$ *2*, there are no user programs per se that are being executed; all such programs are simulated by the event engine in the form of a stream of events that $\mathcal{OSP}$ *2* responds to. There are several advantages to this simulation-based approach. First, events are passed through a so-called *interface layer* (IFL) of $\mathcal{OSP}$ *2* that sits between the event engine and the various $\mathcal{OSP}$ *2* modules in which the code for the system calls resides (see, again, Figure 1.1). The IFL therefore has the opportunity to monitor the execution of system call methods, making sure that the actions taken by these methods are semantically correct. Should an error be detected in a student implementation of a system call method, the IFL can return a meaningful error message to the student. These messages can be a great help to you in debugging your code.

The IFL performs another useful role as far as students (and instructors!) are concerned: it gathers statistics about the system's performance as the event stream is processed. Example statistics collected by the IFL include cpu utilization, number of page faults, and disk-arm movement measured in number of tracks. These statistics are very helpful in gauging the performance of your cpu scheduling algorithm, page replacement scheme, disk scheduling algorithm, etc.

Another advantage of the simulation-based approach is that to debug the OS modules that the student writes there is no need to write and run user-level test programs (as would be the case if you were working with a real OS): the simulator provides the event stream for testing. Moreover, the make-up and

intensity of this event stream generated by the event engine can be adjusted
dynamically by manipulating the *simulation parameters*. For example, if the
instructor has assigned module FILESYS as a project, he can set the simulation
parameters so that the event stream will contain a high percentage of file-system
related events. This yields a simple and effective way of testing the quality of
student programs.

User programs are not the only thing simulated in *OSP 2*. The underlying
hardware is simulated as well and includes a CPU, disk, system clock, hardware
timer, and interrupt vector. The simulated hardware of *OSP 2* is described fully
in Section 1.4.

OSP 2's **Microkernel Architecture.**   An interesting topic in operating-
system design is the *monolithic kernel* versus *microkernel* architecture distinc-
tion. Here the term "kernel" is used to refer to that portion of the operating system that runs in *kernel mode*: the more privileged mode of execution,
as compared to *user mode*, where executing code has access to system data
structures and services. Getting back to the monolithic-versus-microkernel dis-
tinction, a monolithic kernel groups together all operating-system functionality
into a single process while a microkernel assigns only a few essential functions
to the kernel, including address spaces, interprocess communication, and basic scheduling. The microkernel approach is also typified by well-encapsulated
module boundaries for basic services with well-defined interfaces.

As depicted in Figure 1.1 and described above, *OSP 2* is hierarchically structured, consisting of three main layers: the event engine, the IFL, and the student
modules. Once control enters a student module, the system can be considered
to be in kernel mode. Since there are no actual user programs in *OSP 2*, replaced instead by a stochastic simulation of user threads in the form of an event
stream, there is no user mode in *OSP 2* to speak of. Therefore, the file system,
task-management subsystem, virtual memory-management subsystem, etc. run
in kernel mode.

Because of *OSP 2*'s pure object-oriented design, all OS subsystems, including the primitive ones dealing with activities such as thread scheduling and
interprocess communication, are encapsulated in modules (classes) with well-
defined method interfaces. The kind of architecture adopted by *OSP 2* is sometimes referred to as modified microkernel architecture.

1.3 *OSP 2* Organization

OSP 2 comprises a number of projects that may be assigned to students as programming assignments. Each project involves the implementation of a separate Java package consisting of one or more Java classes and their associated methods. Because of their role as potential programming assignments, we shall often refer to these packages as **student packages** or **student projects**. It should be understood, however, that reference implementations of these packages are part of the standard *OSP 2* distribution and must be in place for the system to function normally (unless the reference implementation of a package has been replaced by a student implementation). Each student package is responsible for managing its own class of system resources, as described in the following:

DEVICES: Handles I/O requests for secondary storage devices such as disk drives.

FILESYS: Implements the file system including basic file operations and directory structures.

MEMORY: Manages physical and virtual memory using techniques such as paging and segmentation.

RESOURCES: Manages abstract resources of the system using deadlock detection and deadlock avoidance algorithms.

TASKS: Controls the creation and deletion of tasks, each of which is a container for a set of threads and their associated resources.

THREADS: Responsible for creating, killing, dispatching, suspending, and resuming threads, the fundamental units of execution in *OSP 2*.

PORTS: Implements an interprocess communication facility that allows threads to send messages to each other.

To illustrate how student projects are organized, consider the MEMORY module of *OSP 2*. This module corresponds to the Java package osp.Memory and contains the classes PageFaultHandler, PageTableEntry, and FrameTableEntry, among others. Each of these classes is kept in its own .java file: PageFaultHandler.java, PageTableEntry.java, FrameTableEntry.java, etc. For the MEMORY project, students are expected to implement the various classes associated with these files.

At the heart of *OSP 2* is the **Event Engine**, the event-based simulator that drives the execution of the student packages. The events generated by the event engine are calls to methods in student packages, representing system calls (e.g. create a task, write a file) or hardware interrupts (e.g. disk interrupt, page fault). Collectively, they simulate the behavior of a stream of executing programs in a multiprogramming operating-system environment.

There is also a layer that sits between the event engine and the student layer, the so-called **Interface Layer** or *IFL*. The IFL monitors the execution of the student packages for the purpose of catching semantic errors in student code (and subsequently producing intelligible error or warning messages), and for gathering performance statistics. Thus, the IFL can be viewed as a protective "wrapper" around the student packages. The logical structure of $\mathcal{OSP}$ 2 is depicted in Figure 1.1.

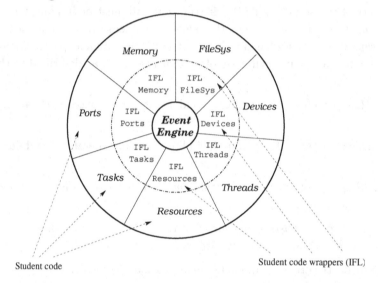

Figure 1.1   The logical structure of $\mathcal{OSP}$ 2.

1.4 Simulated Hardware in $\mathcal{OSP}$ 2

The `Hardware` and the `Interrupts` packages of $\mathcal{OSP}$ 2 model the hardware-oriented aspects of the simulated multiprogramming operating system. `Hardware` consists of four Java classes, which we now describe.[1]

CPU: This class models the CPU of the simulated machine. It defines one method, `interrupt()`, which is used to generate an interrupt with the given type (e.g. disk interrupt, page fault). The interrupt vector supported by the `Interrupts` package is described later in this section.

---

[1] Note that all the methods of the `Hardware` and `Interrupts` packages are declared as `final`, meaning that they cannot be subclassed. This is done for object-oriented design reasons: you should think of these classes as "perfect" or that, conceptually, they should have no subclasses. Many of the methods contained in other $\mathcal{OSP}$ 2 packages are also declared to be `final` for the same reason.

`Disk:` This class represents a hard disk attached to the system and is declared as follows:

`public class Disk extends Device;`

It implements methods that provide access to the physical characteristics of the disk and its current state of operation. The methods in this class are:

⋄ `final public int getPlatters()`
Returns the number of platters.

⋄ `final public int getTracksPerPlatter()`
Returns the number of tracks per platter.

⋄ `final public int getSectorsPerTrack()`
Returns the number of sectors per track.

⋄ `final public int getBytesPerSector()`
Returns the number of bytes per sector.

⋄ `final public int getRevsPerTick()`
Returns the number of revolutions per tick.

⋄ `final public int getSeekTimePerTrack()`
Returns the average time it takes to move the head to the adjacent track.

⋄ `final public int getHeadPosition(int track)`
Returns the position of the disk head, i.e., the cylinder where the head is parked.

These methods might be used for implementing I/O schedulers; see Scheduling of Disk Requests, Chapter 6, for more information about $\mathcal{OSP}$ 2 devices.

`HClock:` This class represents the hardware clock. It can be used to access the current simulation time using the following method:

⋄ `public final static long get()`
Returns current simulation time.

`HTimer:` This class represents the hardware timer. If set to a positive integer, a timer interrupt will occur after that many (simulated) clock ticks. This class provides the following methods:

⋄ `public final static void set(int time)`
Sets timer. Time is relative to the current time. If `time` is zero or negative, timer interrupts are disabled.

◇ public final static long get()
Returns time left until the timer interrupt. Returns a negative number
if timer interrupts are disabled.

The Interrupts package of $\mathcal{OSP}$ 2 consists of one Java class, which is important for several student projects.

InterruptVector: This class represents the hardware register called the **interrupt vector**. It contains information about the interrupt that just occurred. Interrupt handlers check the interrupt vector for the information about the interrupt so that they can properly handle the interrupt. Not all parts of the interrupt vector are relevant to every kind of interrupt. For instance, for timer interrupts, only the type of the interrupt (i.e., that it came from the timer device) is important. On the other hand, for a disk interrupt, the relevant information also includes the IORB (I/O Request Block; see Section 1.6) that caused the interrupt. For a page fault, the relevant information includes the thread and the page that caused the interrupt, etc. The student is supposed to set and query the appropriate parameters of the interrupt vector depending on the type of interrupt. The methods provided by this class are:

◇ final static public void setInterruptType(int newInterruptType)
Sets the type of the interrupt: PageFault, DiskInterrupt, or Timer-
Interrupt; see GlobalVariables for more details.

◇ final static public int getInterruptType()
Returns the type of the interrupt.

◇ final static public ThreadCB getThread()
Returns the thread that caused the interrupt.

◇ final static public void setThread(ThreadCB thread)
Sets the thread that is about to cause the interrupt. In this way, other
modules can query the interrupt vector to find out which thread caused
the interrupt.

◇ final static public PageTableEntry getPage()
Returns the page that caused the interrupt (pagefault).

◇ final static public void setPage(PageTableEntry newPage)
Sets the page that caused the interrupt. In this way, other modules can
query the interrupt vector to find out which page has cause the page
fault.

◇ final static public void setReferenceType(int referenceType)
Sets the reference type of a memory interrupt, i.e., MemoryRead,
MemoryWrite, or MemoryLock; see GlobalVariables.

◇ `final static public int getReferenceType()`
Returns the type of memory reference that caused the interrupt.

◇ `final static public Event getEvent()`
Returns the event that caused the interrupt.

◇ `final static public void setEvent(Event newEvent)`
Sets the event that is about to cause the interrupt.

The hardware components listed above are *provided* by the $\mathcal{OSP}\,2$ system and are not to be implemented by the student. In contrast, $\mathcal{OSP}\,2$ also has hardware, notably the **memory management unit** (or **MMU**), that is part of a student package, module MEMORY. $\mathcal{OSP}\,2$ memory management is discussed in Chapter 5.

1.5 Utilities

The utilities package contains a number of classes that are needed purely for simulation support. It also provides a class, `GlobalVariables`, that is required by the student packages, and several other "utility" classes that assist students in implementing their projects.

The class `GlobalVariables` comprises a number of variables that define the nature of a memory reference (e.g. `MemoryWrite`), interrupt types (e.g. `TimerInterrupt`), and method return status (e.g. `SUCCESS` and `FAILURE`). It also defines constants such as `NONE` and `SwapDeviceID`. The former represents a common return value used for integer objects (e.g. the value returned when a free frame is not found) and the latter is the device number of the swap device.

All of these constants are integers and *must* be referred to using their symbolic names. For debugging, however, it is often useful to know what the corresponding numeric values are. This is accomplished with the help of the following methods:

◇ `final static public String printableStatus(int status)`
Returns the printable representation of the following constants:

– `ThreadReady` – status of a ready-to-run thread.

– `ThreadRunning` – status of a running thread.

– `ThreadWaiting` – status of a waiting thread. (There are multiple levels of waiting, so this status is printed as `ThreadWaitingX`, where `X` is the waiting level. See Chapter 4 for details.)

- **ThreadKill** – status of a killed thread.

- **TaskLive** – status of a live task.

- **TaskTerm** – status of a killed task.

- **PortLive** – status of a live communication port.

- **PortDestroyed** – status of a destroyed communication port.

This method is useful for debugging. For instance, if you need to find out
the status of a thread, you might want to display that status on the screen.
But status is an integer, which does not hold much information for a human
reader. The method `printableStatus()` will convert such an integer into,
say, `ThreadReady` (a string).

◇ **final static public String printableRequest(int request)**
Returns human-readable representations of request constants, which are:

- **MemoryRead** – Memory read request (in `refer()`).

- **MemoryWrite** – Memory write request (in `refer()`).

- **MemoryLock** – Memory lock request (in `lock()`).

- **FileRead** – File read request (in `read()`).

- **FileWrite** – File write request (in `write()`).

◇ **final static public String printableDevice(int device)**
Returns human-readable representations for devices, which are:

- **SwapDeviceID** – the number of the swap device.

- **Disk1, Disk2, Disk3, Disk4** – the disk devices.

◇ **final static public String printableInterrupt(int interrupt)**
Returns human-readable representations for interrupts, which are:

- **PageFault** – Pagefault interrupt.

- **DiskInterrupt** – Disk interrupt.

- **TimerInterrupt** – Timer interrupt.

◇ **final static public String printableRetCode(int retcode)**
Returns human-readable representations of method return-codes. The supported return-codes are:

- **SUCCESS** – successful completion.

- **FAILURE** – unsuccessful completion.

– `NotEnoughMemory` – returned by the page-fault handler when it cannot find a frame to satisfy a page fault.

⋄ `static public String userOption`
This variable is set using the command line option `-userOption`. It can be used to pass a parameter to the student program when $\mathcal{OSP}$ 2 is invoked from command line. This variable is not used internally by the simulator and its use is solely up to the student's discretion.

Other useful classes in the `Utilities` package include:

`MyOut`: The methods in this class can be used to insert messages into the $\mathcal{OSP}$ 2 **system log** for debugging purposes. The system log tracks system events as they occur and messages inserted into the log by students are inserted in chronological order with other system events. The following methods are provided:

⋄ `final public synchronized static void print(Object where, String msg)`
Prints a message to the system log. The argument `where` must be an object from which the package and the class from where `print` is called can be derived. If `print()` is called from a non-static method, then the `where` argument should be *this* (the Java keyword that denotes the context object); otherwise, if `print()` is invoked from within a static method, then the `where` argument should be a string-object of the form `"osp.packageName.className"`. For instance,

`MyOut.print("osp.Tasks.TaskCB", "Hello World!");`

⋄ `final public synchronized static void error(Object where, String msg)`
Prints an error message to the system log and terminates $\mathcal{OSP}$ 2. The format of the `where` argument is the same as before. This method can be used to halt execution of $\mathcal{OSP}$ 2 when a bug is discovered; further execution of $\mathcal{OSP}$ 2 under these circumstance is probably not useful under the circumstances. The `error()` method also causes a stack trace and the current $\mathcal{OSP}$ 2 snapshot to be included in the log for debugging purposes.

⋄ `final public synchronized static void checkCondition(boolean condition, Object where, String msg)`
Similar to `error()` except that the error message is printed and $\mathcal{OSP}$ 2 is terminated only if the boolean `condition` is `false`.

⋄ `final public synchronized static void warning(Object where, String msg)`

Similar to `print()` except that a *warning* message is printed to the log. Unlike `error()` and `checkCondition()` (but like `print()`), the execution of *OSP 2* can proceed after this method is called. Like method `error()`, a snapshot and a stack trace are included in the system log. This method can be used by the student to check conditions that are not necessarily fatal to the execution, but are still undesirable and must be fixed.

◇ `final public synchronized static void snapshot()`
Although `error()`, `warning()`, and `checkCondition()` can be used to obtain the current *OSP 2* snapshot, the `snapshot()` method can be used to insert a snapshot into the system log at any time, not necessarily when a warning or an error condition is detected.

`GenericList`: This class provides the following methods for maintaining doubly linked lists of objects:

◇ `public GenericList() implements GenericQueueInterface`
A constructor that creates an empty list.

◇ `public GenericList(Object obj)`
A constructor that creates a list and initializes it with a given object.

◇ `public final int length()`
Returns the length of the list.

◇ `public final boolean isEmpty()`
Returns true if the list is empty, false otherwise.

◇ `public final synchronized void insert(Object obj)`
Inserts an object at the beginning of the list.

◇ `public final synchronized void append(Object obj)`
Appends an object to the end of the list.

◇ `public final synchronized Object remove(Object obj)`
Removes the specified object from the list and returns the object. Null, if the object is not found.

◇ `public final synchronized Object appendToCurrent(Object obj)`
Inserts the object `obj` into the list after the current item in the list. The current item is set by the enumerators (see below) as they traverse the list (after each call to `nextElement()`).

◇ `public final synchronized Object prependAtCurrent(Object obj)`
Inserts the object `obj` into the list before the current item in the list. The current item is set by the enumerators (see below) as they traverse the list (after each call to `nextElement()`).

⋄ `public final synchronized boolean contains(Object obj)`
Returns true if the specified object is in the list, false otherwise.

⋄ `public final synchronized Object removeHead()`
Removes the object at the head of the list and returns the object. Null, if the list is empty.

⋄ `public final synchronized Object removeTail()`
Removes the object at the tail of the list and returns the object. Null, if the list is empty.

⋄ `public final synchronized Object getHead()`
Returns the object at the head of the list without removing the object.

⋄ `public final synchronized Object getTail()`
Returns the object at the tail of the list without removing the object.

⋄ `public final synchronized Enumeration forwardIterator()`
An iterator is a general Java mechanism for dealing with collections such as sets and lists. A forward iterator returns an object of class `Enumeration` (a standard Java class), which can then be used to conveniently traverse the list. For instance,

```
GenericList list;
.....
Enumeration enum = list.forwardIterator();
while(enum.hasMoreElements()) {
    Object obj = enum.nextElement();
}
```

Each call to `nextElement()` advances the current pointer in the list. The current pointer is the point of insertion for the previously described methods `appendToCurrent()` and `prependAtCurrent()`.

⋄ `public final synchronized Enumeration forwardIterator(Object first)`
Works like `forwardIterator()` but starts the iteration from the first occurrence of the specified object in the list.

⋄ `public final synchronized Enumeration backwardIterator()`
Similar to `forwardIterator()` but traverses the list backwards.

⋄ `public final synchronized Enumeration backwardIterator(Object first)`
Like `forwardIterator(Object first)` but traverses the list backwards.

GenericQueueInterface: The GenericQueueInterface that GenericList
implements contains the following methods:

⋄ public int length();
  Returns the number of elements in the queue.

⋄ public boolean isEmpty();
  Returns true if the queue is empty, false otherwise.

⋄ public boolean contains(Object obj);
  Returns true if the queue contains object obj, false otherwise.

This interface mandates only the methods that $\mathcal{OSP}$ 2 itself uses internally.
For classes that use this interface you might need to define additional methods, such as insertion into the queue and deletion of queue members.

1.6 $\mathcal{OSP}$ 2 Events

Like any other operating system, $\mathcal{OSP}$ 2 is *event-driven*. When a thread executes an I/O operation, it blocks until the I/O completes. When one threads
needs to communicate with another, it sends a message and might decide to
block itself until a response arrives. When a thread blocks, we say that it is
waiting for an **event** to occur (like the completion of an I/O operation or
message delivery) so that the thread may continue its execution.

In a typical operating system, events are represented by some kind of **event**
data structure. A thread that wishes to block itself, or, more generally, to be
notified about the completion of an event, executes a suspend() operation on
that event, which places the thread on the event's **waiting queue**. The event
"happens" when some other thread (a user or a system thread, depending on
the type of the event) announces that the event has taken place. For example,
in the case of an I/O operation, a disk interrupt will cause the disk-interrupt
handler to execute and the handler eventually will announce the completion of
the I/O event. In $\mathcal{OSP}$ 2, an event is an object and such an announcement is
made by executing the notifyThreads() method associated with the event. As
a result, threads waiting on the event are unblocked by the operating system
and can continue their execution.

In $\mathcal{OSP}$ 2, events are represented by the Event class. A basic event has
an id, which serves to distinguish this event from other events and a **waiting
queue**. Thus, an event provides the means for suspending threads when they
have to wait, and subsequently locating them when they are to be resumed.

In practice, the Event class is almost always subclassed before it is used.
This is because threads are usually interested in very specific kinds of events

rather than just generic events. For example, a thread is suspended because it has to wait for an I/O operation to complete or a page to be swapped in, or because it is suspended on a communication port until a message arrives. Thus, *OSP 2* treats memory pages, I/O request blocks (IORBs), and communication ports as events in the sense that all these classes extend the class `Event`.

The `Event` class provides the methods necessary for maintaining the waiting queue, and these methods can be used on pages, ports, and IORBs when these are used in their capacity as events. The methods provided by class `Event` are as follows:

◇ `public void addThread(ThreadCB thread)`
Add the specified thread to the waiting queue of the event. No checks are performed to ensure that the thread is not already on the queue.

◇ `public void removeThread(ThreadCB thread)`
Remove the specified thread from the queue. If the thread is not found, return silently.

◇ `public boolean contains(ThreadCB thread)`
Return true if the thread is on the waiting queue for this event, false otherwise.

◇ `public int getNumberOfThreadsWaiting()`
Returns the length of the waiting queue.

◇ `public GenericList getThreadList()`
Returns the waiting queue itself.

◇ `public ThreadCB getHead()`
Returns the thread at the head of the waiting queue or the null object.

◇ `public void notifyThreads()`
Resumes all threads on the waiting queue (i.e., executes `resume()` on each one of them) and empties the queue. It is quite possible that some threads on the waiting queue have been destroyed while waiting. In this case, `notifyThreads()` simply removes the destroyed threads from the queue as executing `resume()` on such a thread would be an error.

Several projects in *OSP 2* make extensive use of events and we will refer back to this section when necessary.

1.7 *OSP 2* Daemons

The implementation of certain functions of an OS can be facilitated through the use of daemons: special system threads that run periodically and perform "work" specified by the user. In *OSP 2*, such work might include proactive swapping out of dirty memory pages, as required by some memory-management algorithms, and deadlock detection.

Daemon support in *OSP 2* is provided by the Daemon class and the interface DaemonInterface. To use a daemon, one creates an object in a class that implements DaemonInterface and then registers this object with the system. The following statements declare a class of daemons whose only job is to insert a notice in the system log:

```
class MyDaemon implements DaemonInterface
{
    public void unleash(ThreadCB thread)
    {
        MyOut.print(this, "My daemon executed at time: "
                        + HClock.get());
    }
}
```

The only mandatory method in this class is **unleash**, which should contain the code you want the daemon to execute. For instance, in case of a deadlock-detection daemon, a method should be provided that executes the appropriate deadlock-detection algorithm. This method is called by *OSP 2* when it wakes up the daemon.

Defining a daemon is your responsibility. You also need to register it with the system and provide three things: the name of the daemon (for easy identification of the daemon in a system trace), a concrete daemon object to call, and the amount of time that should pass between invocations of the daemon. This is typically done when *OSP 2* begins executing, inside the init() method that exists in the main class of each student package. Here is an example of registering a daemon:

```
Daemon.create("My own daemon", new MyDaemon(), 20000);
```

The first argument can be an arbitrary string. The second is an object of the daemon class defined earlier. The third argument tells *OSP 2* that the daemon should be periodically woken up after every 20,000 ticks.[2] You can create several

---

[2] *OSP 2* does not guarantee that it will wake up the daemon exactly after the specified number of ticks, but it will try to wake it up as soon as possible after the specified interval.

daemons if several periodic jobs need to be performed by the module that you
are implementing. Typically the requirement to use daemons would be part of
the assignment given out by your instructor, but you might also decide to use
them on your own, based on your understanding of the problem.

1.8 Compiling and Running Projects

A student project assignment consists of several files:

1. `Demo.jar`, which contains a demo version of $\mathcal{OSP}\,2$. It can be used to
   get a general idea of how $\mathcal{OSP}\,2$ works, to familiarize yourself with the
   graphical interface and command-line options of the system, and to create
   configuration files for running $\mathcal{OSP}\,2$ with different parameters.

2. Template files, each of which contains the necessary import statements, the
   class header of the public class to be implemented, and the headers of the
   public methods that must be implemented by the student. For instance,
   for the THREADS project, the template files would be

   a) `ThreadCB.java`

   b) `TimerInterruptHandler.java`

3. `OSP.jar`, which contains the compiled classes of the $\mathcal{OSP}\,2$ simulator that
   drive the execution of the classes in the student project. When your implementation of the classes in the project is complete, they should be compiled
   and linked with the `OSP.jar` file.

4. A `Makefile` that simplifies the compilation process under Unix-based systems (Solaris, Linux, Free BSD, etc.).

5. The `Misc` subdirectory, which includes two files:

   a) `params.osp`

   b) `wgui.rdl`

   The first file contains the parameters that will drive the simulation and the
   second file is a configuration file for the GUI. You should not edit either of
   these files manually. In fact, there is no reason to touch `wgui.rdl` at all,
   unless you are not satisfied with the overall look of the graphical interface
   :-). However, you might want to run $\mathcal{OSP}\,2$ with different parameters
   and create a new configuration file derived from `params.osp`. The only
   recommended way of doing this is to change the parameters through the
   GUI of the demo version of $\mathcal{OSP}\,2$ and then save the new parameters in a

new file. A GUI panel that lets the user change the simulation parameters is shown in Figure 1.2.

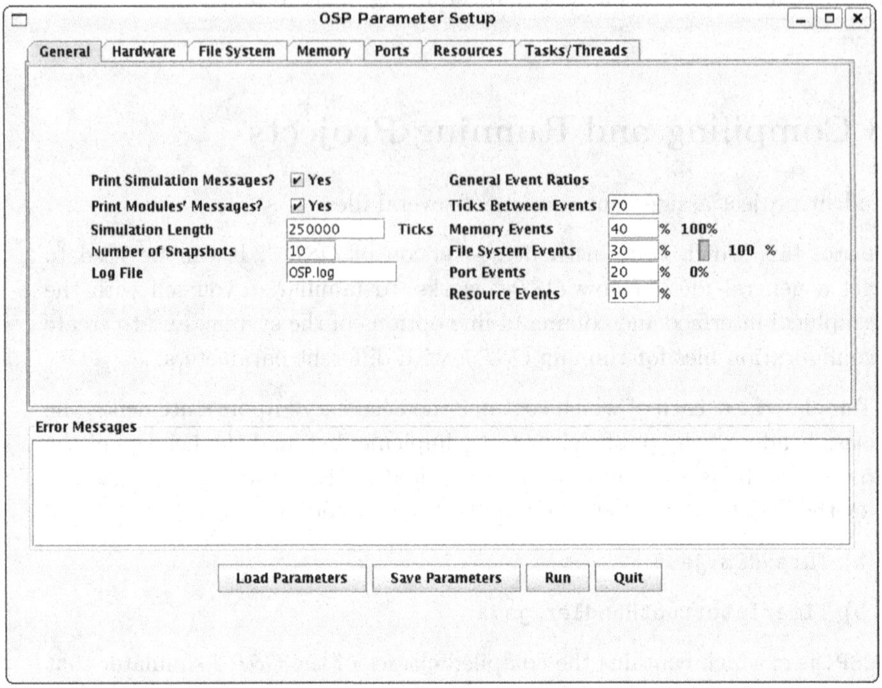

Figure 1.2 Panel for changing $\mathcal{OSP}$ 2 simulation parameters.

Java settings. $\mathcal{OSP}$ 2 requires JDK 1.5 or a later version. To run and compile $\mathcal{OSP}$ 2 you must first make sure that Java is properly set up on your machine and that your personal configuration files are set appropriately. This simply means that the environment variable PATH is set appropriately. For Windows, this variable should be set in the autoexec.bat file or through the control panel as follows:

```
set PATH=%PATH%;C:\jdk\bin
```

The second component in this setting should, of course, point to the place where the Java executables are installed and our choice of C:\jdk\bin is merely an example.

For Unix-based systems, the setting depends on the type of the shell used. We show the settings for the two most popular shells: bash and csh. Settings for other shells (such as `ksh`, `sh`, `tcsh`) would be similar to either `bash` or `csh`, the only difference being the name of the configuration file.

To set the `PATH` variable for `bash`, place the following in the `.bashrc` file in your home directory:

```
PATH=/usr/local/bin/jdk:$PATHexport PATH
```

As before, `/usr/local/jdk/bin` is just an example. The actual location of the Java executables can vary.

For `csh`, the `PATH` variable should be set in the file `.cshrc` in your home directory:

```
setenv PATH /usr/local/bin/jdk:$PATH
```

Running the demo program.   To run the demo version of $\mathcal{OSP}$ *2*, simply type:

```
java -classpath .:Demo.jar osp.OSP
```

(use `.;Demo.jar` on Windows).

Some installations of JDK might require that you set the `CLASSPATH` environment variable (this requirement would then be part of the Java installation instructions). In this case, you might need to run $\mathcal{OSP}$ *2* as follows:

```
java -classpath .:Demo.jar:${CLASSPATH} osp.OSP
```

for Unix-based systems and

```
java -classpath .;Demo.jar;%CLASSPATH% osp.OSP
```

for Windows.

Compiling and running the project.   Once your implementation of the project is finished, you are ready to compile and run the system. Here is how to do this.

On Unix-based systems, simply type `make`, and the project will be compiled. To run it without the GUI, type `make run`; with the GUI, type `make gui`; and to run with the debugger type `make debug`. Sometimes `make clean; make` can be helpful if you need to get rid of stale `.class` files and force recompilation of the entire project. That's all! The only caveat is that this must be a version of *GNU make*, which is available on most Unix-based systems, albeit sometimes under different names, such as **gnumake** or **gmake**. To find out it your make-program is a GNU make, type

```
make --version
```

If it does not say that this is GNU make or if it does not understand the --version argument, then it is *not* GNU make, and you should ask the system administrator if this version of the make-program is installed (and under which name). If you cannot locate the appropriate make-program, read on.

Figure 1.3 shows what you can expect when running $\mathcal{OSP}$ 2 with a GUI and Figure 1.4 shows a run without the GUI.

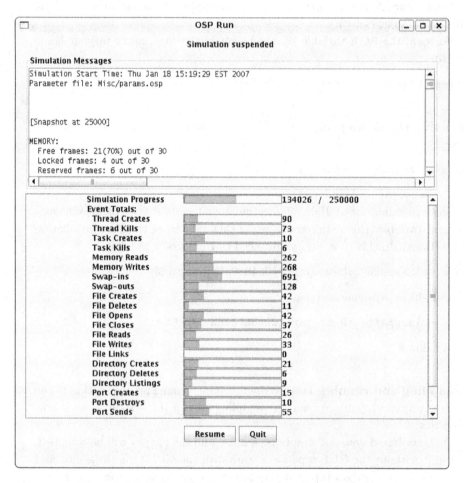

Figure 1.3 An $\mathcal{OSP}$ 2 run with a graphical interface.

The following commands can be used to compile and run $\mathcal{OSP}$ 2 on a Unix-based system:

```
javac -g -classpath .:OSP.jar: -d . *.java
java -classpath .:OSP.jar:. osp.OSP
jdb -classpath .:OSP.jar:. osp.OSP
```

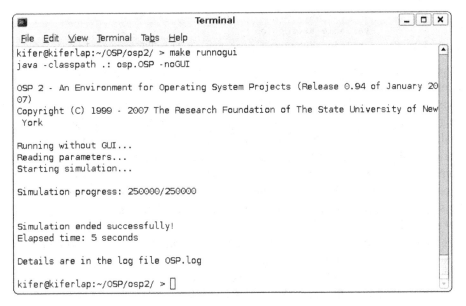

Figure 1.4 An $\mathcal{OSP}$ 2 run without the GUI.

The only difference under Windows is that one has to replace ":" with ";". The first command compiles the project, the second runs it, and the third runs it under the Java debugger.[3] Running $\mathcal{OSP}$ 2 with the Java debugger can be excruciatingly slow, so you should try this only if you need to trace the execution of your program or examine it in some other way that the debugger provides.

Again, some installations of JDK might insists that you set the CLASSPATH environment variable and attach it to the -classpath argument as explained earlier.

$\mathcal{OSP}$ 2 **command-line options.** You can run $\mathcal{OSP}$ 2 with certain command-line options. Here is the full list of options:

```
     -help - lists all command-line options
    -noGUI - runs the simulator without the GUI
-paramFile - use the next argument as the parameter file
  -guiFile - use the next argument as GUI configuration file
```

---

[3] Some Java distributions for Linux have problems with running the debugger due to broken shell scripts. When run, the debugger will complain that it cannot load certain libraries. To fix this, you must set the environment variable LD_LIBRARY_PATH to something like /usr/local/jdk/lib/i386:$LD_LIBRARY_PATH. You might have to do some experimentation to find out the exact path.

```
-userOption - use the next argument to set the global
              variable userOption
  -debugOn - includes debugging messages in the OSP system log
```

Among these, only -userOption, -noGUI, and -paramFile are useful for student projects. The first option, -userOption, allows you to pass a string argument to the student program from the command line. As a result, the string argument specified on the command line becomes the value of the global variable userOption. This can be used, for example, when experimenting with different project implementations, based, perhaps, on different algorithms, and a command-line option is needed to indicate which algorithm to execute. This option can also be used to invoke debugging code that is normally hidden. The second option, -noGUI, runs *OSP 2* without the GUI, which saves time. *OSP 2*'s GUI is very useful as a tool for setting the simulation parameters, but apart from that it is just a very fancy progress bar and, as such, is intended to distract serious people from doing work.

The second useful option, -paramFile, can be used to run *OSP 2* with alternative parameter files, which can be helpful for debugging. The use of -debugOn option is not recommended for student projects. It is mainly a tool for debugging *OSP 2* itself, and the messages it produces can be confusing to someone who is not familiar with the source code of the system. Apart from that, with this option turned on, the OSP system log can be in excess of 30M, which might be a problem on shared file systems.

Here is an example of how to specify command-line arguments to the make command under Unix:

```
make run OPTS="-paramFile my-other-param-file.osp -noGUI"
```

For Windows and for those Unix users who do not trust makefiles, the same effect can be achieved as follows:

```
java -classpath .:OSP.jar osp.OSP
     -paramFile my-other-param-file -noGUI
```

(This command should be typed on one line.)

1.9 General Rules of Engagement

This section describes important general conventions about writing code for student projects.

1.9.1 A Day in the Life of an $\mathcal{OSP}$ 2 Thread

A key concept in $\mathcal{OSP}$ 2 is the *thread*, the schedulable and dispatchable unit of execution in $\mathcal{OSP}$ 2. Threads are simulated in $\mathcal{OSP}$ 2 by the event engine. That is, the event engine, using a certain "stochastic model", semi-randomly decides how many threads to create, how long each of them will live, and what services they will request of the OS while they are alive. A request-of-service by a thread is represented in the event engine by an event corresponding to a call to a method in one of the $\mathcal{OSP}$ 2 modules. For example, if $\mathcal{OSP}$ 2 wants to simulate a request by a thread to read a certain file, an event is created that will eventually result in a call to method do_read() of class OpenFile of package FILESYS.

A key point that we will emphasize numerous times in this book is that the threads that $\mathcal{OSP}$ 2 simulates represent the behavior of user programs or applications. In a typical computing environment, an application program performs some useful work for a user. To do so, the application requests services from the operating system, such as memory allocation, the use of the CPU, management of files, etc. The user sees the results of the work performed by the application, but the details of how the services are implemented by the operating system are normally hidden from the user.

In $\mathcal{OSP}$ 2 you have to take the opposite view: your concern is the operating system itself, and the user applications are faceless programs that you know nothing about. The only time you become aware of these programs is when they—or more precisely the simulated $\mathcal{OSP}$ 2 threads representing the behavior of these programs—request services from you, the operating system. The aim of each of student project is to implement a well-defined service, such as memory or thread management, that might be requested by a typical application. When a simulated $\mathcal{OSP}$ 2 thread requests a service from the OS, it suddenly becomes "real": a call is made to one of the methods in your project and the simulated computation becomes live computation of one of the methods that you implemented.

$\mathcal{OSP}$ 2 has a modular, object-oriented design with clear interfaces. Every student project implements a particular service. The implementation of the classes needed to complete each project is under the student's control. For each class, the student is required to implement certain methods and in doing so can augment the class with any number of auxiliary methods or variables. The student is also provided with a set of methods to operate on the "built-in" data structures of the class (which are represented as private fields in the IFL layer). In some cases, it becomes necessary to obtain services from other parts of the system, which is also done through the published interfaces.

It is important to keep in mind that if you are assigned, say, the memory-management project, MEMORY, then you are responsible for implementing all the necessary functionality as defined by the project description. $\mathcal{OSP}$ 2 will not attempt to provide any memory-related service, leaving everything to you. However, like a Big Brother, it is watching and is very keen on reporting errors.

When implementing a project, only the interfaces described in that project's description can be used. Method calls and classes that you might find in the description of other projects will not work and are likely to result in a compilation error. This is the result of the method-name obfuscation described in Section 1.9.4, which is performed to prevent corruption of the internal system state.

1.9.2 Convention for Calling Student Methods

One of the most important tasks of the $\mathcal{OSP}$ 2 simulator is to verify the actions performed by student code for semantic correctness and to provide meaningful error messages and warnings. This error checking is performed by the **interface layer** of $\mathcal{OSP}$ 2 (or IFL). The IFL contains wrapper methods that validate the state of the system before and after student code is executed. Because of these wrappers, a special convention for naming and invoking methods must be followed when implementing an $\mathcal{OSP}$ 2 project. To make the discussion concrete, consider the THREADS package, which is responsible for thread-management tasks such as thread creation. There is both a Java class for threads in the IFL, called `IflThreadCB` (the CB stands for "control block"), and a Java class for threads in the student package, simply named `ThreadCB` (i.e. without the `Ifl` prefix). Moreover, `ThreadCB` is a *subclass* of `IflThreadCB` and both of these classes implement methods for thread creation (among others), with the IFL method serving as a protective "wrapper" for the student-layer method.

To distinguish these thread-creation methods, the one defined in the superclass is simply called `create()`, while the one in the subclass is called `do_create()`, i.e. the corresponding method name in the student package is prepended with the prefix `do_`. In general, we have the following naming convention.

> *Methods in the $\mathcal{OSP}$ 2 API that are to be implemented by the student have the naming schema* `do_name`, *where* `name` *is the name of the wrapper in the IFL.*

There is an exception to this rule, namely the methods `atError()` and `atWarning()`, which are introduced below.

This convention has several ramifications that the student must be aware of when implementing a project. These are best understood by considering the flow of execution in $\mathcal{OSP}$ 2 when an event is generated by the event engine and subsequently "handled" by the appropriate classes in the IFL layer and student package. Five main points of control can be identified within this execution flow; see also Figure 1.5.

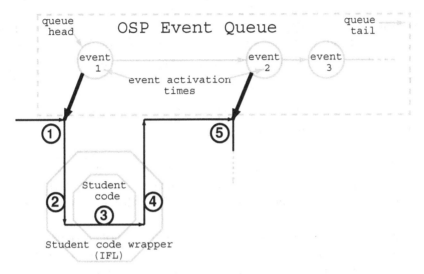

Figure 1.5 Execution flow for handling an event.

1. The event engine selects the event at the head of the "event queue" for execution. The event is actually a call to one of the student methods although control must go through the IFL. Assume, for the sake of discussion, that the selected event is a call to the `create()` thread method. In this case, the event engine calls `create()` in the IFL.

2. The IFL performs some bookkeeping for the purpose of detecting possible errors in, and for monitoring the performance of, the student's implementation of `create()` and then calls `do_create()` in the student layer.

3. The student implementation of `do_create()` performs the requested action.

4. Control returns to `create()`, which verifies that the actions taken by the student code were correct. If the student code executed incorrectly, an error message is written to the simulation log and simulation halts.

5. Assuming the student code executed correctly, simulation proceeds to the next scheduled event on the event queue.

Students should therefore adhere to the following additional naming convention:

> *When* calling *a method named* name *in this or another package, call the method* name, *i.e. without the "do_" prefix.*

In contrast, as noted above, when *implementing* a method named name, students will actually implement the method do_name.

Note also that *the student implementation should never directly refer to the classes defined in the IFL layer.* For instance, even though the method dispatch() is defined in the class IflThreadCB, it is inherited by ThreadCB and it should be called as ThreadCB.dispatch() rather than IflThreadCB.dispatch().

1.9.3 Static vs. Instance Methods

When you receive a project assignment that contains the templates of the methods to be implemented, you will notice that some methods are static (i.e., they apply to class objects) and some methods (those that do not have the static keyword attached) work on instance objects.

This division of the project methods into static and instance methods comes from the differences in their function. For example, the method do_dispatch() is static in class ThreadCB, because it makes no sense to call it on any particular thread: the thread to be dispatched is not known at the time of the call and, in fact, it is the job of the do_dispatch() method to find such a thread and give it control of the CPU, as described in Chapter 4.

On the other hand, methods do_resume() and do_suspend() in ThreadCB are *not* static: they are called on specific thread objects, because the job of these methods is to resume or suspend the threads on which the methods are called. As usual in Java, the context object of a non-static method is accessible through the variable this.

Therefore, when reading the description of each method in the project, it is important to be aware of whether this method is static or an instance method.

1.9.4 Obfuscation of Method and Class Names

Chapters 3 through 8 describe the classes and methods that comprise the various student projects. For each project, the student implementation may require services implemented in other parts of $\mathcal{OSP}$ 2 and must call the appropriate methods to obtain these services. Methods needed for one project, however, are not necessarily needed for another. In some cases, incorrect use of methods that belong to other packages might even corrupt the internal state of the system.

To prevent the student implementation from incorrectly using public methods that are not required for the given project, the names of these methods are changed in that project by a special "obfuscater" program. For example, the method `isFree()` of class `FrameTableEntry` is available in project MEMORY, but it is obfuscated away and will cause a compilation error if it is used by methods in project THREADS.

1.9.5 Possible Hanging After Errors

When $\mathcal{OSP}$ 2 detects an error in a student program, it prints information about the error and then tries to terminate. Graceful termination, however, is not always possible because $\mathcal{OSP}$ 2 is a multi-threaded application and termination of some of the active threads might depend on student code (whose behavior cannot be predicted). It is therefore possible that, after printing an error message, $\mathcal{OSP}$ 2 may hang; in this case the system must be terminated by the user.

1.9.6 Possible Exceptions After the End of Execution

On very rare occasions you might see exceptions that occur after the end of a run of the simulator. This is nothing to worry about, however, as it does *not* indicate a problem with your program. The reason for these exceptions is that when the designated simulation time runs out, $\mathcal{OSP}$ 2 tries hard to stop all the currently active Java threads. Unfortunately, it is not possible to terminate threads immediately, so a thread may continue to run for a short while even though some of the vital system objects may have already been destroyed. In such situations, `NullPointerException` and other exceptions can occur.

1.9.7 General Advice: How to Figure it Out

When you begin an $\mathcal{OSP}$ 2 project, it is important to understand the specifications of the various student projects contained in the following chapters, and how your implementation fits into the big picture. Perhaps, it is best to state what this manual is *not*:

1. It is *not* intended to replace the textbook.

2. It is *not* intended to teach you the basic concepts in operating systems.

3. It is *not* intended to guide you every step of the way to the completion of

your project.

Instead, the description of a student project provides a complete description of the API that you can use to implement the project and a description of the functionality of each method in the project. The manual does not explain how to put the pieces of the puzzle together—this is for you to figure out based on your understanding of the subject.

The best advice is: think logically. In these projects *you are implementing parts of an operating system*, which is probably very different from the kind of programming you have done in the past. If you are in doubt about whether or not it is appropriate for your implementation to take a certain action, consider whether you would like it if the OS on your desktop behaved this way. For example, suppose you are implementing a thread scheduler and at certain point in the program you have to deal with the situation where no threads are left to schedule. Should you leave the CPU idle or create and run a dummy thread, thereby wasting computing resources? The answer should become obvious if you just ask yourself the simple question: "Would I want my home computer to behave this way?"

1.10 System Log, Snapshots, and Statistics

During a run, $\mathcal{OSP}$ 2 prints messages in the system log. Each message describes a specific event that occurred during execution. Messages that come from the simulator are prefixed with `Sim:`; those that come from student packages other than the project-assignment module(s) are prefixed with `Mod:`; and those that come from the project you are currently implementing are prefixed with `My:`.

Periodically $\mathcal{OSP}$ 2 dumps **snapshots** of the system state into the log file. These snapshots are primarily intended for performance checking and debugging. A snapshot contains a complete dump of main memory, the status of all page tables, the status of all threads, including the queues they are in, and the status of all communication ports.

In addition, the snapshot provides statistics such as CPU utilization, **average service time** (also known as **average turnaround time**) of an I/O request and a thread, the average number of tracks swept on each device per I/O request, and the **average normalized service time**. The last of these describes the average relative delay suffered by each thread, and is determined by the following formula:

$$\frac{\Sigma_i \dfrac{\text{CPU time used}(\text{thread}_i)}{\text{turnaround time}(\text{thread}_i)}}{\text{total number of threads}}$$

where the sum is over all threads (dead or alive). This is a better measure of performance than the average turnaround time, and this statistic should be kept as high as possible (but, of course, it cannot exceed 1).

It should be noted that some entries in the system log can have fairly long lines, so to view the log it may be necessary to use a viewer with horizontal scroll capability. For example, if you are running $\mathcal{OSP}\ 2$ with a parameter file that specifies long page tables (say, more than 64 pages), then you can expect to need to use a scrollable viewer. Most text editors provide this capability.

1.11 Debugging

There is no special-purpose debugger for $\mathcal{OSP}\ 2$, but there are a few things that can help. Generally, errors in student code can be divided in two categories:

1. Errors that cause Java exceptions.

2. Semantic errors, such as an incorrect action taken in response to a simulator request. Examples include the failure to maintain the correct status of a thread (e.g., `ThreadWaiting` instead of `ThreadRunning`) or replacing a dirty page without first swapping it out to the swap device.

Errors of the first kind are much easier to fix since they can be identified with the help of a Java debugger, such as `jdb`. For example, a Java debugger can be used to determine where the exception `NullPointerException` has occurred. In all likelihood, Java exceptions are due to errors in student code. If an exception takes place in $\mathcal{OSP}\ 2$ code, it does not necessarily mean that the student code is correct; rather, it likely means that $\mathcal{OSP}\ 2$ has failed to catch the problem early enough to generate a meaningful error message to guide you to the real problem.

Apart from tracking down exceptions, Java debuggers are not very useful for debugging $\mathcal{OSP}\ 2$ projects, especially for finding semantic mistakes in student code. This is because such an error might be detected by $\mathcal{OSP}\ 2$ thousands of instructions after the erroneous action was performed by the student program and using the debugger trace facility to track down the source of the error might wear you down before the first signs of a problem begin to show up. Therefore, the following procedure is recommended for finding and fixing semantic problems.

System log. When $\mathcal{OSP}\ 2$ detects a semantic error, it tries to come up with as clear an explanation as possible. When an error or a warning is issued, the log file (OSP.log, unless specified differently in the configuration file) will contain a message of the form <<Error>>, <<Assertion>>, or <<Warning>>, which are easy to find with an editor. When $\mathcal{OSP}$ 2 terminates, it tells you if one of these conditions was encountered or if it terminated successfully.

In case of a problem, the best way to understand what might have happened is to trace back the messages in the system log. For instance, if an error message says that you are trying to dispatch a thread that is waiting on some event that has not occurred yet, you should trace back and see when the thread was suspended on that event and what was the sequence of events that happened since. You might discover, for example, that your program is placing threads on the ready queue that, in reality, are not ready to execute. Likewise, if $\mathcal{OSP}$ 2 complains that there is a discrepancy between what it perceives to be the dirty/clean status of a page and the value of the dirty bit set for this page by the student program, tracing the system log might reveal that, say, this page has just been swapped in but your program did not reset the dirty bit to *false*.

$\mathcal{OSP}$ 2 generates a log by default, unless tracing is turned off. However, the log messages thus generated are typically not sufficient by themselves to debug errors in your code. This is because $\mathcal{OSP}$ 2 cannot know what is actually happening inside student code and it is therefore necessary to put the execution of your program in the context of the overall execution of $\mathcal{OSP}$ 2. This can be achieved with the help of the methods in the class MyOut, which were discussed earlier. Moreover, it is useful to keep in mind that the toString() method of all major classes in $\mathcal{OSP}$ 2 is set up in a printer-friendly manner. For example, executing

```
MyOut.print(this,
            "The " + thread + " is suspended on " + event);
```

where thread is an object of class ThreadCB and event is an object of class Event will produce output that looks like this:

```
My:  2534.5533 [Threads.ThreadCB] The Thread(15:32/RU)
     is suspended on Event(3)
```

Thus, no special care is needed to produce a readable representation of $\mathcal{OSP}$ 2 objects. The header of the $\mathcal{OSP}$ 2 system log provides a brief explanation of the printable representation of various objects. For instance, in the above representation for a thread, Thread(15:32/RU), the first number (15) is the thread id, the second (32) is the Id of the task the thread belongs to, and RU is the code that represents the current status of the thread (ThreadRunning in this case).

Error and warning hooks.   In addition to MyOut, the main class of every student project has the following pair of methods:

◇ public static void atError()

◇ public static void atWarning()

The first method is called when an error or a condition violation is detected by
$\mathcal{OSP}$ 2, and the second is called right after $\mathcal{OSP}$ 2 issues a warning message.
Normally, the bodies of these methods are empty, *and this is how you should
leave them when you submit your program.* However, during debugging you can
put arbitrary code there. Most useful would be code that prints the status of the
relevant variables in your program. Note that whenever a condition violation,
error, or warning occurs, $\mathcal{OSP}$ 2 prints the full stack trace that indicates the
sequence of method calls that led to the problem.

System snapshot. $\mathcal{OSP}$ 2 also produces a **system snapshot** when a condition violation or error occurs. The snapshot conveys the status of memory
allocation, the status of each task and thread in the system, etc. This information can be compared with the status of the system per your implementation
and the system log can be consulted to determine where the discrepancy arises.
When $\mathcal{OSP}$ 2 prints out a warning, no snapshot is added to the log by default.
This is because warnings tend to come in large numbers and this can lead to
an unmanageably large number of snapshots in the log. However, you can include the `snapshot()` method of class `MyOut` in the body of the `atWarning()`
method of the main class of your project and produce a snapshot in this way. (It
is recommended to print a snapshot only on the first warning, since subsequent
snapshots are not likely to shed any more light on the problem.)

Execution stack trace.   Another important resource for debugging $\mathcal{OSP}$ 2
projects is the execution stack trace provided by the Java virtual machine when
a Java exception occurs. Here is an example of such a trace:

```
java.lang.NullPointerException
  at osp.Threads.ThreadCB.do_kill(ThreadCB.java:195)
  at osp.IFLModules.IflThreadCB.kill(IflThreadCB.java:634)
  at osp.IFLModules.IflThreadCB.killOldThreads(IflThreadCB.java,
     Compiled Code)
  at osp.IFLModules.CallbackThreadKill.voidCallback(IflThreadCB.java,
     Compiled Code)
  at osp.EventEngine.EventCallback.Activate(EventCallback.java,
     Compiled Code)
  at osp.EventEngine.EventEngObj.ActivateChildren(EventEngObj.java,
     Compiled Code)
  at osp.EventEngine.EventEngObj.Activate(EventEngObj.java,
     Compiled Code)
  at osp.EventEngine.EventDriver.go(EventDriver.java:114)
  at osp.EventEngine.EngineThread.run(EngineThread.java:61)
```

The trace says that a `NullPointerException` has occurred in method do_kill() of class ThreadCB at source code line 195. Going down the trace, we can see the sequence of method calls that led to the error: do_kill() was called by kill() of IflThreadCB, etc. The most important information here is the line number where the error occurred.[4]

OSP 2 prints a similar trace in the system log when an error or a warning is issued. For instance,

```
Sys: 36360 <<Warning!>> [Threads.ThreadCB]
  After do_kill(Thread(36:1/KL)): CPU is idle,
  but there are ready threads
  ready queue = (89:3,115:2,130:2,141:3,142:5)
  at osp.IFLModules.IflThreadCB.idleCPUwarning(IflThreadCB.java,
    Compiled Code)
  at osp.IFLModules.IflThreadCB.kill(IflThreadCB.java, Compiled Code)
  at osp.Tasks.TaskCB.do_kill(TaskCB.java, Compiled Code)
  at osp.IFLModules.IflTaskCB.kill(IflTaskCB.java, Compiled Code)
  at osp.IFLModules.IflTaskCB.killOldTasks(IflTaskCB.java, Compiled Code)
  at osp.IFLModules.CallbackTaskKill.voidCallback(IflTaskCB.java,
    Compiled Code)
  at osp.EventEngine.EventCallback.Activate(EventCallback.java,
    Compiled Code)
  at osp.EventEngine.EventEngObj.ActivateChildren(EventEngObj.java,
    Compiled Code)
  at osp.EventEngine.EventEngObj.Activate(EventEngObj.java, Compiled Code)
  at osp.EventEngine.EventDriver.go(EventDriver.java:114)
  at osp.EventEngine.EngineThread.run(EngineThread.java:61)
```

The trace appears after the warning message. In this case, we must look deeper in the trace to find out what happened. The top line of the trace says that the warning was issued by method idleCPUwarning() of class IflThreadCB, which was called by kill(), the system wrapper for the do_kill() method, which is part of a student project (refer back to Section 1.9.2 for the information about the naming conventions for methods that are implemented as part of student projects). The trace further says that the method IflThreadCB.kill() was in turn called by the method do_kill() of class TaskCB, which was called by IflTaskCB.kill(). It takes a little bit of analysis and understanding of the functionality of the different system calls to realize what happened: the task Task(1/L) has been destroyed by the system call TaskCB.kill(), which caused the destruction of all the threads that belong to that task. In particular, just after thread Thread(36:1/KL) was killed, the system detected that the CPU was idle even though some ready-to-run threads were present in the system. Thus, the cause of the warning is most probably the failure of the student implementation to call the dispatch() method at the end of do_kill().

---

[4] Line-number information is not always provided, unless you run the system using the debugger.

Obfuscation and stack traces. Unfortunately, the obfuscation that $\mathcal{OSP}\,\mathcal{2}$ employs to prevent inappropriate calls to certain methods diminishes the value of execution stack traces, because the names of some method calls listed in a trace might be unintelligible. However, even with name obfuscation, the trace often contains enough information to be useful. Here is an example of an obfuscated trace:

```
java.lang.NullPointerException
    at osp.IFLModules.IflDevice.enqueueIORB(IflDevice.java:283)
    at osp.FileSys.OpenFile.do_read(OpenFile.java:421)
    at osp.IFLModules.IflOpenFile.read(IflOpenFile.java:415)
    at osp.Memory.PageFaultHandler.a(PageFaultHandler.java:395)
    . . .
```

In the last line, the real name of the method `osp.Memory.PageFaultHandler.a` was obfuscated and became unrecognizable (there is no method called `a` in the source code). However, it is still clear that the error occurred while a call to the method `enqueueIORB` was made from within the `read` method, which was executed on a file.

1.12 Project Submission

The manner by which you submit your $\mathcal{OSP}\,\mathcal{2}$ projects is determined by the instructor. The following instructions apply if your instructor chooses to use the automatic project submission system of $\mathcal{OSP}\,\mathcal{2}$.

First, you will have to supply your email address to the instructor, who will prepare an account for you. The email address identifies you to the system. You must use the same address in all your interactions with the submission system.

The submission system provides three functions, which are available as links from the project submission page. The URL of this page will be supplied to you by your instructor. The functions are as follows:

1. *Change of password.*
   Clicking on this link will let you change your password. Your initial password will be mailed to you when the instructor sets up your account.

   After you change your password and then try to submit a project, you might see the "authorization has failed" dialog box. This happens when the browser tries to use your old password. It is not a problem, however, because clicking "OK" in the dialog box lets you re-enter the correct password.

2. *Password reminder.*

If you forget your password or if you did not receive the initial password for some reason, you should click on this link. First, you will get email with a link to a servlet. Clicking on this link will have the following effect:

◇ Your password will be changed to some random string.

◇ You will get your new password by email.

If the new password is hard to remember, you can use the "Change of password" function to change your password.

If you do not click on the aforesaid servlet link, your password will not be changed. It should be noted that the password-reminder function can be used only within intervals of at least four hours.

3. *Project submission.*
   When you are ready to submit your project assignment, click on the "Submit assignment" link on the project submission page. After authentication, you will be presented with a form where you will be asked to enter the project name and the *.java files that comprise your program. The system then copies the sources over to the server and compiles them. If successful, the sources stay on the server (so that they can be checked by the instructor and his or her teaching assistants) and the compiled class files are sent back to your browser as an applet. Next, you will have to run this applet (by clicking on appropriate buttons). If you are happy with the results, click on the submission button. The simulation run will then be sent to the server (again, so that the instructor can check it for errors).

   Note that some browsers do not give a warning when a non-existing file is being sent to the server. In some cases (e.g. when the file is actually a directory name) the browser might even hang. Therefore, it is important to make sure that you send the correct *.java files to the server.

   You should keep in mind that the instructor might set up the submission process in such a way that your project would have to be run with several parameter files. When the first run is finished, you should press the *Submit* button and then the *Next* button. If there are more parameter files to be considered, a new applet will start. When this is finished, submit the output and hit *Next* again. When your project has been run with all the parameter files, you will receive a confirmation and the main project-submission page will be displayed.

   Finally, some browsers might issue a security exception when you try to run the submission applet. You will see this exception in the Java console of the browser (we recommend that you always run the submission applet with the Java console open). If this happens, you should place the file

.java.policy in your home directory. This file should contain the entry

```
grant {
    permission java.security.AllPermission;
};
```

2

Putting it All Together: An Example Session with OSP 2

2.1 Chapter Objective

Your instructor has assigned you the THREADS project to implement; see Chapter 4. You are new to *OSP 2*. What do you do? In this chapter, we present an example session with *OSP 2* that is intended to give you the guidance and confidence you need to successfully complete your assignment.

2.2 Overview of Thread Management in *OSP 2*

The THREADS project, as the name implies, deals with thread management and scheduling, where threads are the executable and dispatchable units in *OSP 2*. Our example will focus on thread management, in particular, the resumption of a thread from a waiting state. This activity is the responsibility of the method do_resume(), one of the methods you are to implement as part of your implementation of the class ThreadCB.

Thread management involves the notions of thread creation, destruction, suspension, resumption and dispatching; maintaining thread status; and moving threads between different (ready and waiting) queues. Underlying all of this is the notion of a thread *state*, which can be one of ThreadReady, ThreadWaiting, ThreadKill, etc.

An $\mathcal{OSP}$ 2 thread assumes the `ThreadWaiting` state when it enters the pagefault handler or when it executes a blocking system call (e.g., `write()`). The `ThreadWaiting` state is also known as the "level-0 waiting state". While in this state, a thread can again enter the pagefault handler or execute a blocking system call, causing it to enter the level-1 waiting state, represented by the constant `ThreadWaiting+1`. This process can continue indefinitely, leading to arbitrarily nested depths of waiting.

When a thread completes the execution of the pagefault handler or blocking system call, it should be moved up to the next highest waiting level by decrementing its waiting status; in the case of level 0 (`ThreadWaiting`, it should transit to the `ThreadReady` state.

2.3 The Student Method `do_resume()`

As mentioned previously, we will focus our attention during this example session on the method `do_resume()` of class `ThreadCB`. Its code is given in Figure 2.1. Notice the use of the `MyOut` utility to insert student output in the file `OSP.log`. For example, the statement

```
MyOut.print(this, "Resuming " + this);
```

will result in output such as

```
Mod: 63 [Threads.ThreadCB]
        Resuming Thread(0:1/W2)
```

appearing in the log file, indicating that at simulation time 63, thread 0 of task 1 is at waiting-level 2 (`W2`). The tag "`Mod:`" identifies this output as being from a student module, making it easy for you to distinguish your output from $\mathcal{OSP}$ 2's in the log file.

Do_resume() is one of the simplest methods in $\mathcal{OSP}$ 2. All it needs to do is decrement the thread's waiting-level, place it on the ready queue if its new status is `ThreadReady`, and call `dispatch()` so that some thread can be dispatched onto the CPU for execution.

Assuming that you have completed your design and coding of the THREADS project, let us proceed in a step-by-step fashion with the example session.

```
/** Resumes the thread.

Only a thread with status ThreadWaiting or higher can
be resumed.  The status must be set to ThreadReady or
decremented, respectively.  A ready thread should be
    placed on the ready queue.

@OSPProject Threads
*/
public void do_resume()
{
    if(getStatus() < ThreadWaiting) {
    MyOut.print(this,
        "Attempt to resume "
        + this + ", which wasn't waiting");
    return;
}

    MyOut.print(this, "Resuming " + this);

    // Set thread's status.
if (getStatus() == ThreadWaiting) {
    setStatus(ThreadReady);
} else if (getStatus() > ThreadWaiting)
    setStatus(getStatus()-1);

    // Put the thread on the ready queue, if appropriate
if (getStatus() == ThreadReady)
    readyQueue.append(this);

dispatch();
}
```

Figure 2.1 Code for student method do_resume().

2.4 Step 1: Compiling and Running the Project

◇ You have a directory with all the necessary files in it for the THREADS project: ThreadCB.java, TimerInterruptHandler.java, OSP.jar, Makefile, etc.

◇ You have set the environment variable PATH appropriately so that the proper version of JDK (1.5 or newer) will be invoked.

◇ On Unix-based systems, you can use the make command to compile the project. For this example session, we will compile OSP 2 to run without the GUI by issuing the command:

```
make runnogui
```

◇ Problems in compiling? If you think this could be due to stale .class files, type make clean and then make to force recompilation of the entire project.

◇ To now run the project, type:

```
java -classpath .: osp.OSP -noGUI
```

2.5 Step 2: Examining the OSP.log File

Assuming for the moment that you have correctly implemented the THREADS project and $\mathcal{OSP}\,2$ ran successfully to completion without errors, let us now take a look at a relevant snippet from the OSP.log file:

```
Sim: 63 [Memory.PageTableEntry]
        Unlocking Page(12:1/0). New lock count: 0
Sim: 63 [Threads.ThreadCB]
        Entering resume(Thread(0:1/W2))
Mod: 63 [Threads.ThreadCB]
        Resuming Thread(0:1/W2)
Sim: 63 [Threads.ThreadCB]
        Leaving resume(Thread(0:1/W1))
Mod: 63 [Hardware.Disk]
        Device(0) has no pending IORBs to dequeue
```

At simulation time 63, thread 0 of task 1 has exited the pagefault handler and is "resumed" by the student method do_resume(). In this case, this means the thread moves from waiting-level 2 to waiting-level 1.

The log file also contains statistics about tasks and threads generated during our successful run of the THREADS project. It is a good idea to have a look at these too, both to see how well your implementation is performing and to simply get a better understanding of how threads behave in $\mathcal{OSP}\,2$.

```
TASKS and THREADS:
  CPU Utilization: 61.382%
  Average service time per thread: 36180.812
  Average normalized service time per thread: 0.047044374
  Total number of tasks: 4
  Running thread(s): none
  Threads summary: 18 alive
  Among live threads: 0 running
                      6 suspended
                      0 ready
```

```
ready queue = ()
running thread(s) = ()
waiting thread(s) = (97:12,107:13,110:15,111:15,112:15,113:15)
thread(s) in pagefault = (110:15,115:13,124:13)
killed thread(s) = (7:1,15:1,13:1,12:1,10:1,9:1)
```

2.6 Step 3: Introducing an Error into do_resume()

Unfortunately, not all of your runs of $\mathcal{OSP}$ 2 will be as successful as the one above: we all make programming mistakes, whether they be logical errors or simply typographical errors. Let us consider what happens when the latter occurs. In particular, suppose that in do_resume(), instead of typing:

```
} else if (getStatus() > ThreadWaiting)
    setStatus(getStatus()-1);
```

you type:

```
} else if (getStatus() > ThreadWaiting)
    setStatus(getStatus()+1);
```

This is not an uncommon mistake: typing a plus sign when indeed you meant to type a minus sign. What are the consequences of this typo? Well, for one, $\mathcal{OSP}$ 2 will terminate unsuccessfully at simulation time 63 and place the following output in the log file:

```
 Sim: 63
[Threads.ThreadCB]
        Entering resume(Thread(0:1/W2))
Mod: 63 [Threads.ThreadCB]
        Resuming Thread(0:1/W2)
Sim: 63 <<Error!>> [Threads.ThreadCB]
        After do_resume(Thread(0:1/W3)): Thread status is
        ThreadWaiting3; should be ThreadWaiting1

        at osp.IFLModules.IflThreadCB.resume(IflThreadCB.java:1101)
        at osp.IFLModules.Event.notifyThreads(Event.java:130)
        at osp.Devices.DiskInterruptHandler.do_handleInterrupt
            (DiskInterruptHandler.java:114)
        at osp.IFLModules.IflDiskInterruptHandler.handleInterrupt
            (IflDiskInterruptHandler.java:107)
```

```
at osp.Interrupts.Interrupts.interrupt(Interrupts.java:48)
at osp.Hardware.CPU.interrupt(CPU.java:54)
at osp.IFLModules.IflIORB.voidCallback(IflIORB.java:238)
at osp.IFLModules.CallbackDiskInterrupt.voidCallback
   (IflDevice.java:604)
at osp.EventEngine.EventCallback.Activate(EventCallback.
   java:48)
at osp.EventEngine.EventDriver.go(EventDriver.java:119)
at osp.EventEngine.EngineThread.run(EngineThread.java:60)
```

As you can see, the simulator has detected our error! What follows the error message is a dump of the system-call stack which indicates the sequence of method calls that led to the problem. Not surprisingly, $\mathcal{OSP}$ 2's IFL version of do_resume is at the top of the stack, as it was in this "wrapper method" where the error was detected. In an actual debugging situation, you would use this information to isolate and repair the problem in your implementation of the do_resume() method.

To complete our example session, here are the statistics for tasks and threads that can be found in the log file at the end of our unsuccessful run.

```
TASKS and THREADS:
  CPU Utilization: 28.57143%
  Average service time per thread: 63.0
  Average normalized service time per thread: 0.28125
  Total number of tasks: 1
  Running thread(s): none
  Threads summary: 1 alive
  Among live threads: 0 running
                      1 suspended
                      0 ready
  ready queue = ()
  running thread(s) = ()
  waiting thread(s) = (0:1)
  thread(s) in pagefault = (0:1)
  killed thread(s) = ()
```

3

TASKS: *Management of Tasks (a.k.a. Processes)*

3.1 Chapter Objective

The objective of the TASKS project is to teach students about task management in a modern-day operating system and to provide them with a well-structured programming environment in which to implement task-management techniques. To this end, students will be asked to implement the $\mathcal{OSP}\,2$ class TaskCB, the only class of package TASKS. TaskCB stands for *Task Control Block*, the $\mathcal{OSP}\,2$ object used to represent tasks.

3.2 Conceptual Background

Like other modern operating systems, $\mathcal{OSP}\,2$ distinguishes between program execution and resource ownership. The former is captured through the concept of a **thread**, which represents a running program, and the latter is captured using the concept of a **task**. In older operating systems, like traditional Unix, the **process** filled both of these roles; actually, we sometimes use the term "process" as a synonym for task. In $\mathcal{OSP}\,2$, a task serves as a "container" for one or more threads, all executing the same code and sharing the same memory address space. Also associated with a task is a swap file containing an image of the task's address space, other files opened by the task's constituent threads, and the communication ports created by these threads. We say that these resources (memory, ports, files, etc.) are *owned* by the task and *shared* by the task's threads; this explains how the issue of resource ownership is organized around the concept of a task.

Threads are the schedulable and dispatchable units of execution in $\mathcal{OSP}$ 2. They are sometimes referred to as "lightweight processes" for it is much easier in a multiprogramming OS to switch the CPU from one thread to another than from one process to another, due to above-explained separation of program execution and resource ownership in an OS supporting the task/thread doctrine. We will have more to say about threads in the next chapter.

A task can be created or destroyed, newly created threads can be added to a task, and threads are deleted from the owner task's thread list after they are destroyed. There is also a system-wide notion of the **current task**, which is the task that owns the currently running thread. This thread is known as the **current thread** of the task.

In the rest of this chapter we describe `TaskCB`, the only class in the TASKS package. The class diagram of Figure 3.1 puts `TaskCB` in context with related classes.

3.3 Class `TaskCB`

Tasks are represented by the class `TaskCB`, which is the only class to be implemented in the TASKS project. It is defined as follows:

⋄ `public class TaskCB extends IflTaskCB`

The following methods are to be implemented as part of this project:

⋄ `public static void init()`
This method is called at the very beginning of simulation and can be used to initialize static variables of the class, if necessary.

⋄ `public static TaskCB do_create()`
This method creates a new task object and then initializes it properly.

In $\mathcal{OSP}$ 2, creation of a task involves the creation of a task object, allocation of resources to the task, and various initializations. The task object is created using the default task constructor `TaskCB()`. First, a page table must be created using the `PageTable()` constructor, and associated with the task using the method `setPageTable()`. Second, a task must keep track of its threads (objects of type `ThreadCB`), communication ports (objects of type `PortCB`),

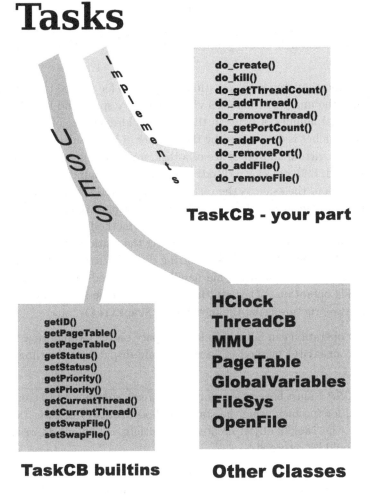

Figure 3.1 Overview of the package TASKS.

and files (objects of type `OpenFile`), which means that the appropriate structures have to be created. $\mathcal{OSP}$ 2 does not have any specific requirements for these data structures, except that they must correctly maintain the inventory of threads, ports, and files attached to the task. Lists or variable-size arrays are good candidates.

Next, the task-creation time should be set equal to the current simulation time (available through the class HClock), the status should be set to TaskLive, and the task priority should be set to some integer value. $\mathcal{OSP}$ 2 does not prescribe what this value should be; it is determined by the requirements of the project and might be specified by the instructor (if, for example, the scheduling strategy implemented in the THREADS project uses task priorities).

The next important step is the creation of the swap file for the task. A swap file contains the image of the task's virtual memory space and thus is equal to the maximal number of bytes in the virtual address space of the task. In $\mathcal{OSP}$ 2 this number is determined by the number of bits needed to specify an address in the virtual address space of a task, and is obtained using the following method: MMU.getVirtualAddressBits(). The name of the swap file is, by convention, the same as the task ID number, and the file itself resides in the directory specified by the global constant SwapDeviceMountPoint. To create the swap file, you should use the static method create() of class FileSys. Then the file has to be opened using the static method open() of OpenFile. The open() method takes a string that represents a full path name of a file and returns a run-time file handle that is used in the read, write, and close file operations. The resulting open-file handle should be saved in the task data structure using the method setSwapFile().

An open() operation can fail due to lack of space on the swap device. In this case the do_create() method of TaskCB should dispatch a new thread and return null.

A task in $\mathcal{OSP}$ 2 must have at least one live thread, so you need to create the first thread for the task using the static method create() of class Thread-CB. Finally, the TaskCB object created and initialized by your do_create() method should be returned.[1]

◇ public void do_kill()
This method is called to destroy a task. First, it should iterate through the list of all live threads of the task and kill() them. (Recall that maintenance of this list is entirely the responsibility of your implementation.) Each time a thread is killed, the do_removeThread() method is called by the THREADS package. The do_kill() method should then iterate over the ports attached to the task and destroy() them as well. Each request to destroy a port will eventually result in a call to your do_removePort() method. The status

---

[1] There is no need to invoke the dispatch() method of ThreadCB in order to schedule a thread to run after the do_create() system call is complete. Since a new thread is created as part of the process of task creation, dispatch() will be called by the create() method of ThreadCB. However, calling dispatch() before leaving do_create() is harmless.

of the task should be set to `TaskTerm` (terminated task) and the memory previously allocated to the task should be released. The latter is accomplished by invoking the method `deallocateMemory()` of class `PageTable` on the page table of the task.

The last resource left to be released by the task is the set of files opened by the various threads of the task and the swap file of the task. The **open files table** of a task is a data structure that should be maintained as part of the implementation of class `TaskCB` and should include all files opened by the threads of the task (which are objects of class `OpenFile`); $\mathcal{OSP}$ 2 does not prescribe how this should be done. To free up this resource, you must `close()` every file in the open files table.

You should keep in mind that each call to `close()` eventually results in a call to your method `do_removeFile()`. However, this might not happen immediately. When you close a file that is the target of an active I/O operation, i.e., an operation that is currently being processed by an external device such as a disk, the file is not closed immediately. Rather, the system will remember that the file needs to be closed and will re-issue the `close()` command when the I/O operation completes. Because of this possible delay, some files of the task can remain open for a period of time even after you perform the `close()` operation on every open file. This means, of course, that calls to your method `do_removeFile()` might be similarly delayed.

Finally, the swap file of the task must be destroyed using method `delete()` of `FileSys`.[2] The argument to this method is the name of the swap file (see the discussion of `do_create()`).

◇ `public int do_getThreadCount()`
This method must return a correct thread count, which must be maintained as part of the implementation of the `do_create()` and `do_kill()` methods.

◇ `public int do_addThread(ThreadCB thread)`
This method is called by other parts of $\mathcal{OSP}$ 2 whenever a new thread is created. The purpose of these calls is to notify `TaskCB` of the creation of a new thread so that the inventory of threads owned by the task can be properly updated. `SUCCESS` is to be returned unless the maximum number of threads for this task has been reached, in which case, `FAILURE` should be returned.

◇ `public int do_removeThread(ThreadCB thread)`
This method is called when a thread is destroyed. The thread should be

---

[2] Closing a file does not deallocate the space; it merely removes the file handle and flushes the data on disk. Deleting a file removes a hard link to the file, and when the number of such links becomes zero, the file space is freed.

removed from the list of threads owned by the task. SUCCESS should be
returned if the thread belongs to the task and FAILURE otherwise.

◇ public int do_getPortCount()
Returns the number of ports owned by the task.

◇ public int do_addPort(PortCB newPort)
This method is called when a new communication port is created by one of
the task's constituent threads. It enables TaskCB to maintain the inventory
of ports that belong to the task. If the maximum number of ports for this
task has been reached, FAILURE should be returned. Otherwise, SUCCESS is
returned.

◇ public int do_removePort(PortCB oldPort)
This method is called when one of the task's communication ports is destroyed. The method should remove the port from the list of ports maintained by TaskCB. SUCCESS is to be returned if the port belongs to the task;
FAILURE otherwise.

◇ public void do_addFile(OpenFile file)
Adds file to the table of open files of the task. The implementation of
the table is entirely up to the student. This method is typically called
by the method open() of class OpenFile (indirectly, through the wrapper
addFile()).

◇ public int do_removeFile(OpenFile file)
Removes file from the table of open files of the task. This method is typically called by the method close() of class OpenFile. It returns SUCCESS if
the file belongs to the task; FAILURE otherwise.

Relevant methods and fields defined in this and other packages.
The following public methods and fields of other classes are useful for implementing the methods of the TASKS project.

◇ public final static float get()   HClock
Returns the current simulation time.

◇ static public int MaxThreadsPerTask   ThreadCB
Maximum allowed number of threads per task.

◇ final static public void dispatch()   ThreadCB
Dispatches a new thread.

◇ public static int MaxPortsPerTask   PortCB
Maximum allowed number of ports per task.

⋄ `final public int destroy()`   PortCB
Destroys the port on which it is called.

⋄ `static public int getVirtualAddressBits()`   MMU
Returns the number of bits needed to specify a virtual address. Can be used
to determine the size of the swap file.

⋄ `final public PageTable getPageTable()`   TaskCB
Returns the page table of the task.

⋄ `final public void deallocateMemory()`   PageTable
Deallocates (frees) the memory used by the task. Called when a task is
terminated. Is invoked on the task's page table.

⋄ `public PageTable(TaskCB ownerTask)`   PageTable
Page table constructor (should be used with the **new** operator). Used to
create a page table object for a newly created task. This object must then
be associated with the task using the `setPageTable()` method.

⋄ `public final static String SwapDeviceMountPoint GlobalVariables`
The mount point for the swap device in the file system. It is the name of
the directory where all swap files live, and is terminated with a slash or
a backslash. The name of the task's swap file is `SwapDeviceMountPoint`
concatenated with the task ID.

⋄ `final public static int create(String name, int size)`   FileSys
Here **name** is the *full path name* of the file and `size` is the desired initial
size in bytes. The size of a file is assumed to always be a multiple of the
disk block size (which is identical to the virtual memory page/frame size).
This method returns SUCCESS if the file is successfully created and FAILURE
otherwise. A `create()` operation can fail if, for example, the device does
not have enough space.

⋄ `final public static void delete(String name)`   FileSys
Deletes the file. (See the description of class **FileSys** for more details about
this method.)

⋄ `final public static OpenFile open(String name,TaskCB task)`
                                                                  OpenFile
Opens the file **name** and returns a file handle for use at run time to read
and write the file.

⋄ `final public int close()`   OpenFile
When invoked on an open file handle, closes the file. Returns SUCCESS if
the file is successfully closed and FAILURE otherwise. A `close()` operation
might fail, for example, if the file has outstanding I/O operations.

⋄ `final static public ThreadCB create(TaskCB task)`   ThreadCB
Creates an active thread for the task supplied as an argument. Returns the
created thread.

◇ `final public void kill()`   ThreadCB
  Destroys the thread. Notice that this method calls your implementation of
  `do_removeThread()` to disassociate the thread from the task.

Summary of Class `TaskCB`

The following table summarizes the attributes of class `TaskCB` and the methods
for manipulating them. These attributes and methods are provided by the class
`IflTaskCB` and are inherited. The methods appearing in the table are more fully
described in Section 3.4.

Identity: The identity of a task is set by the system, but it can be queried with
  the method `getID()`.

Page table: The page table of a task is set with the method `setPageTable()`
  and can be retrieved using `getPageTable()`.

Status: The status of a task is handled using the methods `setStatus()` and
  `getStatus()`.

Priority: The status of a task is handled using the methods `setPriority()`
  and `getPriority()`.

Current thread: Indicates which thread of a task is currently running. The
  methods to query and modify this attribute are `getCurrentThread()` and
  `setCurrentThread()`.

Creation time: The creation time of a task is handled using the methods
  `getCreationTime()` and `setCreationTime()`.

Swap file: A task's swap file is set and retrieved using the methods
  `getSwapFile()` and `setSwapFile()`.

Table of open files: Keeps track of all of the open files of a task, which are
  instances of class `OpenFile`. $\mathcal{OSP}\ 2$ does not impose any requirements to
  how this table is maintained as long as it properly keeps inventory of a
  task's open files. Two methods are used in conjunction with this table:
  `addFile()` and `removeFile()`. Calls to these methods by other packages
  are intended to notify a task as to which files it owns. In addition, when
  a task is destroyed, all its files must be closed. This is performed as part
  of the `do_kill()` method, which must iterate through this table and close
  all the files in it. The `do_`-versions of the `addFile()` and `removeFile()`
  methods are part of the TASKS project. Note that `TaskCB` never calls these
  methods—it *implements* them.

Table of ports: Keeps track of all of the communication ports owned by a task. *OSP 2* does not define a specific variable by which to refer to this table, and the internal data structure used to implement it is entirely up to the student. However, the following methods are defined to manipulate this table: `getPortCount()`, `addPort()`, and `removePort()`. The first indicates how many open ports the task has; the second is used to attach a new port to the task; and the last is used to remove destroyed ports. The `do_`-versions of these methods are part of the TASKS project. `TaskCB` *implements* these methods—it never calls them.

Table of live threads: As with ports, *OSP 2* does not prescribe how this table is to be implemented. However, the following methods are defined to manipulate this table: `getThreadCount()`, `addThread()`, and `removeThread()`. The first method counts the number of live threads owned by the task, the second adds newly created threads to tasks, and the third method removes killed threads. The `do_`-versions of these methods are implemented by the student. These methods are *implemented* by `TaskCB`— they are never called by this class.

3.4 Methods Exported by the TASKS Package

The following is a summary of the public methods defined in the classes of the TASKS package or in its superclasses. These methods can be used in the implementation of this or other student packages. To the right of each method we list the class of the objects to which the method applies. In the case of the TASKS package, all exported methods belong to a single class, `TaskCB`, which inherits them from the superclass `IflTaskCB`. In general, the public methods exported by a student package may belong to more than one class; see, for example, package MEMORY (Section 5.8).

◇ `final public void setPageTable(PageTable table)`   TaskCB
  Sets the page table of the task.

◇ `final public PageTable getPageTable()`   TaskCB
  Returns the page table of the task.

◇ `final public int getStatus()`   TaskCB
  Returns the status of the task. Allowed values are `TaskLive`, for live tasks, and `TaskTerm`, for terminated tasks.

◇ `final public void setStatus(int s)`   TaskCB
  Sets the status of the task.

◇ `final public int getPriority()`   TaskCB
Returns the priority of the task.

◇ `final public void setPriority(int p)`   TaskCB
Sets the priority of the task.

◇ `public ThreadCB getCurrentThread()`   TaskCB
Returns the current thread of the task. The current thread is the thread that will run when the task is made current by the dispatcher.

◇ `public void setCurrentThread(ThreadCB t)`   TaskCB
Sets the current thread of the task.

◇ `final public int getID()`   TaskCB
Returns the ID of the task.

◇ `final public double getCreationTime()`   TaskCB
Returns the task creation time.

◇ `final public void setCreationTime(double time)`   TaskCB
Sets the task creation time to `time`.

◇ `public final OpenFile getSwapFile()`   TaskCB
Returns the swap file of the task.

◇ `public final void setSwapFile(OpenFile file)`   TaskCB
Sets the swap file of task to `file`.

◇ `final public int addThread(ThreadCB thread)`   TaskCB
Adds the specified thread to the list of threads of the given task.

◇ `final public int removeThread(ThreadCB thread)`   TaskCB
Removes the specified thread from the list of threads of the given task.

◇ `final public int getThreadCount()`   TaskCB
Returns the number of threads in the task.

◇ `public final void addFile(OpenFile file)`   TaskCB
Adds `file` to the table of open files of the task. The implementation of the table is entirely up to the student.

◇ `public final void removeFile(OpenFile file)`   TaskCB
Removes `file` from the table of open files of the task.

◇ `final public int addPort(PortCB newPort)`   TaskCB
Adds `newPort` to the list of ports associated with the task.

◇ `final public int removePort(PortCB oldPort)`   TaskCB
Removes `oldPort` from the list of ports owned by the task.

◇ `final public int getPortCount()`   TaskCB
    Returns the number of ports owned by the task.

THREADS: *Management and Scheduling of Threads*

4

4.1 Chapter Objective

Threads are the schedulable and dispatchable units of execution in $\mathcal{OSP}\,2$. The objective of the THREADS project is to teach students about thread management and scheduling in a modern-day operating system and to provide them with a well-structured programming environment in which to implement thread-management and scheduling techniques. To this end, students will be asked to implement the two public classes of the THREADS package: `ThreadCB` and `TimerInterruptHandler`. The former implements the most common operations on a thread, while the latter is a timer interrupt handler that can be used to implement time-quantum-based scheduling algorithms for threads. We begin this chapter with an overview of thread basics.

4.2 Overview of Threads

Multi-threading refers to the ability of an OS to support multiple threads of execution within a single task. There are at least four reasons why it is desirable to structure applications as multi-threaded ones:

Parallel Processing: A multi-threaded application can process one batch of data while another is being input from a device. On a multiprocessor architecture, threads may be able to execute in parallel, leading to more work getting done in less time.

Program Structuring: Threads represent a modular means of structuring an application that needs to perform multiple, independent activities.

Interactive Applications: In an interactive application, one thread can be used to carry out the current command while, at the same time, another thread prompts the user for the next command. This pipelining effect can lead to a perceived increase in the speed of the application.

Asynchronous Activity: A thread can be created whose sole job is to schedule itself to perform periodic backups in support of the main thread of control in a given application.

Concurrency: Threads can execute concurrently. Thus, for example, a server process can service a number of clients concurrently: each client request triggers the creation of a new thread within the server.

We thus see that there is considerable incentive from an application programming perspective for an OS to support multi-threading.

Threads as Independent Entities.   As explained in Chapter 3, the resources available to a thread, such as memory, open files and communication ports, are those belonging to the task to which the thread is affiliated. That is, a task is a container for one or more threads and each of these threads has shared access to the resources owned by the task. There is, however, certain information associated with a thread that allows it to execute as a more or less independent entity:

⋄ A thread execution state (Running, Ready, Blocked, etc.).

⋄ A saved thread context when not running. This context includes the contents of the machine registers when it was last running; in particular, every thread has its own, independent program counter.

⋄ An execution stack.

⋄ A certain amount of per-thread static[1] storage for local variables.

⋄ Access to the memory and resources of its container task; it shares these resources with the other threads in that task.

---

[1] Not to be confused with the Java keyword `static` used to define a variable as a class variable or a method as a class method.

It is worth taking time to emphasize the implications of this last item. All
the threads of a given task reside in the same address space and have access
to the same data. Consequently, when one thread modifies a piece of data, the
effect of this change is visible to the other threads should they subsequently
decide to read this data item. If one thread opens a file with read access, the
other threads in the same task will also be able to read from this file. It is thus
imperative that when programming a multi-threaded application, the actions
of the threads be carefully coordinated; otherwise conflicts could easily arise
that could hinder the threads from performing their desired computation.

Scheduling Algorithms for Threads.   As previously noted, threads are
the schedulable units of execution in $\mathcal{OSP}\ 2$ and any other OS that supports
threads. This represents a shift from older operating systems like traditional
Unix in which processes played this role.[2] Thread scheduling is an integral part
of multiprogramming: when the currently executing thread becomes blocked
waiting for some event to occur, this represents a golden opportunity for the
OS to perform a context switch so that a ready-to-run thread can be given
control of the CPU. In this way, the CPU is kept busy most of the time,
thereby increasing its utilization.

So what are the kinds of events that threads may block on? These include
I/O interrupts and software signals. It should be noted, however, that an OS
can decide to perform a context switch any time it is convenient, again for
the purpose of improving system performance. Convenient in this case means
any time control resides within the OS, and include occasions such as timer
interrupts and system call invocations.

The question you must now ask yourself is which thread should the OS
schedule next when a context switch is to take place? The decision taken here
is critical; it can significantly impact a variety of performance-related measures,
such as:

CPU utilization: the percentage of time the CPU is kept busy (not idle).

Throughput: the number of jobs or tasks processed per unit of time.

Response time: the amount of time needed to process an interactive command.
Typically one is interested in the average response time over all commands.

Turnaround time: The amount of time needed to process a given task. Includes
actual execution time plus time spent waiting for resources, including the
CPU.

---

[2] Modern Unix implementations, like SUN's Solaris, IBM's AIX, and Linux, do, of
course, support threads.

The answer to the question as to which thread to schedule next lies in the **CPU scheduling algorithm** the OS implements. A variety of scheduling algorithms have been proposed in the literature and they can be classified along the following lines:

Emphasis on response time vs. CPU utilization. Algorithms of the former kind can be thought of as user-oriented and those of the latter kind as system-oriented.

Preemptive vs. nonpreemptive. A preemptive algorithm may interrupt a thread and move it to the ready-to-run queue, while in the nonpreemptive case, a thread continues to execute until it terminates or blocks on some event. Several preemptive algorithms preempt a thread after it has finished up its "slice" or quantum of CPU time.

Fair vs. unfair. In a fair algorithm, every thread that requires access to the CPU eventually gets time on the CPU. In the absence of fairness, **starvation** is possible and the algorithm is said to be unfair in this case.

Choice of selection function. The selection function determines which thread, among the ready-to-run threads, is selected next for execution. The choice can be based on priority, resource requirements, or execution characteristics of the thread such as the amount of elapsed time since the thread last got to execute on the CPU.

We now briefly describe some of the more common scheduling algorithms that have been proposed. In describing these algorithms, we assume the existence of a **ready queue** where ready-to-run threads lie in wait for the CPU.

First-Come-First-Served (FCFS) As the name indicates, threads are serviced in the order they entered the ready queue. This is probably the simplest scheduling algorithm that has been proposed and has the tendency to favor long, CPU-intensive threads over short, I/O-bound threads.

Round Robin. Like FCFS but each thread gets to execute for a length of time known as the **time slice** or **time quantum** before it is preempted and placed back on the ready queue. Time slicing can be used to allow short-lived threads, corresponding to interactive commands, to get through the system quickly, thereby improving the system's response time.

Shortest Thread Next (STN). This is a nonpreemptive policy in which the thread with the shortest expected processing time is selected next. Like round robin, it tends to favor I/O-bound threads. The scheduler must have an estimate of processing time to perform the selection function.

Shortest Remaining Time (SRT). This is a preemptive version of STN in which the thread with the shortest expected remaining processing time is selected next. SRT tends to yield superior turnaround time performance compared with STN.

Highest Response Ratio Next (HRRN). A nonpreemptive algorithm that chooses the thread with the highest value of the ratio of $R = \frac{w+s}{s}$, where R is called the response ratio, w is the time spent waiting for the CPU, and s is the expected service time. Favors short threads but also gives priority to aging threads with high values for w.

Feedback. This algorithm, sometimes referred to as "multi-level round robin" utilizes a series of queues, each with their own time quantum. Threads enter the system at the top-level queue. If a thread gains control of the CPU and exhausts its time quantum, it is demoted to the next lower queue. The lowest queue implements pure round robin. The selection function chooses the thread at the head of the highest non-empty queue. Thus this algorithm penalizes long-running threads since each time they use up their time quantum, they are demoted to the next lower queue.

Priority-Driven Preemptive Scheduling. The basic idea of this scheme is that when a thread becomes ready to execute whose priority is higher than the currently executing thread, the lower-priority thread is preempted and the processor is given to the higher-priority thread. Thread priorities may be computed statically (threads have a fixed priority that never changes) or adjusted dynamically (a thread's priority begins at some initial assigned value and then may change, up or down, during the thread's lifetime). The priority-driven preemptive approach to thread scheduling is especially important in operating systems that support **real-time** threads or processes, such as Linux, Unix SVR4, and Windows 2000/XP/Vista.

The rest of this chapter describes each class in the package THREADS in detail. These classes are placed in a larger context in the class diagram given in Figure 4.1.

4.3 The Class ThreadCB

ThreadCB stands for **thread control block**; it is a class that contains all the structures necessary for maintaining the information about each particular thread. This class is defined as follows:

◊ public class ThreadCB extends IflThreadCB

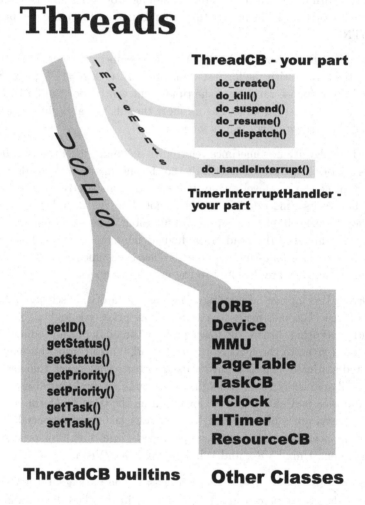

Figure 4.1   Overview of the package THREADS.

Like other classes that belong to student projects, this class defines methods that start with do_ and that are wrapped with similarly named methods in class IflThreadCB. Before discussing the required functionality of the methods in ThreadCB we need to look deeper into the nature of $\mathcal{OSP}$ 2 threads.

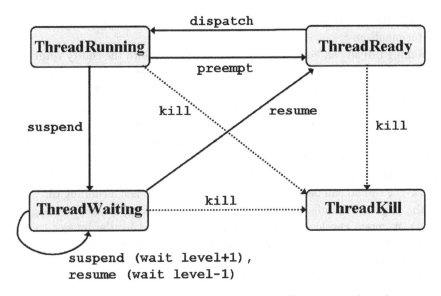

Figure 4.2 The state transition diagram for $\mathcal{OSP}$ 2 threads.

State transitions.   Thread management is concerned with two main issues: the life cycle of a thread (i.e., **creation** and **destruction** of threads) and maintaining thread status and moving threads between different queues and CPU (**suspension, resumption**, and **dispatching**). Therefore, to understand thread management in $\mathcal{OSP}$ 2 it is important to understand the different states a thread can be in and how state transitions take place. Figure 4.2 illustrates this issue.

When a thread is first created, it enters the ready state (`ThreadReady`), which means it must be placed on the queue of ready-to-run threads. $\mathcal{OSP}$ 2 does not prescribe how this queue is supposed to be organized and it is entirely up to the student implementation, unless the instructor has specific requirements.

From then on, two things can happen: a ready-to-run thread can be **scheduled to run** (and **dispatched**) and gain control of the CPU (and thus change its status to `ThreadRunning`), or it can be **destroyed** (or **killed**) and change its status to `ThreadKill`.

A thread can be dispatched only if it has the status `ThreadReady`, but a live thread (i.e., one that has status *other than* `ThreadKill`) can be killed in any state, not only in the ready state. One sad thing about $\mathcal{OSP}$ 2 threads is that they never die of natural causes: they either get destroyed by somebody else or self-destroy. In other words, there is no separate system call to terminate a thread normally and there is no special state to denote normal thread termination.

A running thread can be preempted and placed back into the **ready queue** or it can be suspended to the **waiting state**. The latter can happen due to a pagefault or when the thread executes a blocking system call, such as an I/O operation or a communication (sending or receiving a message). $\mathcal{OSP}$ 2 does not place any restrictions on the way the ready queue is implemented, so you should use your own design. However, your instructor may have specific requirements to how scheduling is to be done. In this case, some designs might be much better than others.

An $\mathcal{OSP}$ 2 thread can be at several levels of waiting. When a running thread enters the pagefault handler or when it executes a blocking system call (e.g., `write()`), it enters the level 0 waiting state represented by the integer constant `ThreadWaiting`. Level 1 waiting state is represented by the constant `ThreadWaiting+1`, etc.

A thread is not always blocked when it enters a waiting state. For instance, when a thread causes a pagefault or executes a `write()` operation on a file, its waiting state signifies that in order to continue execution of the user program the thread needs to wait until the pagefault or the system call is finished. In other words, the thread switches hats: it leaves the user program and becomes a system thread. A system thread might do some work needed to process the request and then it might execute another system call. At this point, it would enter the waiting state at level 1, which signifies that the original thread has to wait for two system calls to complete. If the second system call is blocking (e.g., involves I/O), the execution of the thread will block until the appropriate event happens (e.g., the I/O completes).

To illustrate this process, consider processing of a pagefault (Chapter 5). When a pagefault occurs, the thread enters the level 0 waiting state, executes a page replacement algorithm and then makes a system call to `write()`. When the `write()` call starts execution, the thread's waiting level is bumped up to 1. After assembling a proper I/O request to the swap device, the thread will suspend itself on a blocking event, to wait for the I/O. At this point, the thread will be in state `ThreadWaiting+2`. When the I/O is finished, the `resume()` method is executed on the thread and it drops into the level 1 waiting state. When the `write()` system call is about to exit, another `resume()` is executed and the thread's wait level drops to 0 (i.e., its state becomes `ThreadWaiting` again). Next, while still in the pagefault handler, the thread would execute the `read()` system call and go into the waiting state at levels 1 and 2, similar to the `write()` call. When the `read()` operation is finished, the ensuing `resume()` operations will drop the thread to level 0 again. At this point, the pagefault handler performs some record-keeping operations (see Chapter 5), executes a resume() operation and exits. This causes the thread to change its status from ThreadWaiting to ThreadReady.

In sum, an $\mathcal{OSP}$ 2 thread can be suspended to several levels of depth by executing a sequence of nested suspend() operations. When all the corresponding events happen, the resume() method is called on the thread, which decreases the wait level by 1. When all the events on which the thread is suspended occur, the thread goes back into the ThreadReady state.

Context switching.   Passing control of the CPU from one thread to another is called **context switching**. This has two distinct phases: **preempting** the currently running thread and **dispatching** another thread. Preempting a thread involves the following steps:

1. Changing of the state of the currently running thread from ThreadRunning to whatever is appropriate in the particular case. For instance, if a thread loses control of the CPU because it has to wait for I/O, then its status might become ThreadWaiting. If the thread has used up its time quantum, then the new status should become ThreadReady. Changing the status is done using the method setStatus() described later.

   This step requires knowing the currently running thread. The call MMU. getPTBR() (described below) lets you find the page table of the currently scheduled task. The task itself can be obtained by applying the method getTask() to this page table. The currently running thread is then determined using the method getCurrentThread().

2. Setting the **page table base register** (PTBR) to null. PTBR is a register of the memory management unit (a piece of hardware that controls memory access), or MMU, which always points to the page table of the running thread. This is how MMU knows which page table to use for address translation. In $\mathcal{OSP}$ 2, PTBR can be accessed using the static methods getPTBR() and setPTBR() of class MMU.

3. Changing the current thread of the previously running task to null. The current thread of a task can be set using the method setCurrentThread().

When a thread, t, is selected to run, it must be given control of the CPU. This is called **dispatching** a thread and involves a sequence of steps similar to the steps for preempting threads:

1. The status of t is changed from ThreadReady to ThreadRunning.

2. PTBR is set to point to the page table of the task that owns t. The page table of a task can be obtained via the method getPageTable(), and the PTBR is set using the method setPTBR() of class MMU.

3. The current thread of the above task must be set to t using the method `setCurrentThread()`.

In practice, context switch is performed as part of the `dispatch()` operation, and steps 2 and 3 in the first list above can be combined with steps 2 and 3 of the second list.

In the degenerate case, when the running thread t is suspended and no other thread takes control of the CPU, consider it as a context switch from t to the imaginary "`null` thread". Likewise, if no process is running and the dispatcher chooses some ready-to-run thread for execution, you can view it as a context switch from the `null` thread to t.

Events.   Before going on you must revisit Section 1.6, which describes the `Event` class.

The state transition diagram shows that to a large extent thread management is driven by two operations: `suspend()` and `resume()`. The suspend operation places a thread into a waiting queue of the event passed as an argument (and increases the wait level) and the resume operation decreases the wait level and, if appropriate, places it into the queue of ready-to-run threads (in which all threads are in the `ThreadReady` state). All this is accomplished using the `Event` class discussed in Section 1.6. Note that, as described earlier, a thread can execute several suspend operations on different events, so it might find itself in different waiting queues. The thread will be notified about the completion of these events in the order opposite to that in which the `suspend()` operations were performed. After all the relevant events have occurred, the thread is free to execute again and is placed on the ready queue.

Only the first method in class `Event`, `addThread()`, is really necessary for the THREADS project, but other methods might be useful for debugging (and, of course, they are necessary for other $\mathcal{OSP}$ *2* projects).

Methods of class `ThreadCB`.   These are the methods that have to be implemented as part of the project. Their implementation requires support from other parts of OSP in the form of the methods that can be called from within `ThreadCB` to accomplish a specific objective. We discuss these methods as part of the required functionality and then give a summary of these methods in a separate section.

⋄ `public static void init()`
  This method is called once at the beginning of the simulation. You can use it to set up static variables that are used in your implementation, if necessary. If you find no use for this feature, leave the body of the method empty.

⋄ `public static ThreadCB do_create(TaskCB task)`

The job of this method is to create a thread object using the default constructor `ThreadCB()` and associate this newly created thread with a task (provided as an argument to the `do_create()` method). To link a thread to its task, the method `addThread()` of class `IflTaskCB` should be used and the thread's task must be set using the method `setTask()` of `IflThreadCB`.

There is a global constant (in `IflThreadCB`), called `MaxThreadsPerTask`. If this number of threads per task is exceeded, no new thread should be created for that task, and `null` should be returned. `null` should also be returned if `addThread()` returns `FAILURE`. You can find out the number of threads a task currently has by calling the method `getThreadCount()` on that task.

If priority scheduling needs to be implemented, the `do_create()` method must correctly assign the thread's initial priority. The actual value of the priority depends on the particular scheduling policy used. $\mathcal{OSP}$ 2 provides methods for setting and querying the priority of both tasks and threads. The methods are `setPriority()` and `getPriority()` in classes `TaskCB` and `ThreadCB`, respectively.

Finally, the status of the new thread should be set to `ThreadReady` and it should be placed in the ready queue.

If all is well, the thread object created by this method should be returned.

It is important to keep in mind that each time control is transferred to the operating system, it is seen as an opportunity to schedule a thread to run. Therefore, regardless of whether the new thread was created successfully, the dispatcher must be called (or else a warning will be issued).

⋄ `public void do_kill()`

This method destroys threads. To destroy a thread, its status must be set to `ThreadKill` and a number of other actions must be performed depending on the current status of the thread. (The status of a thread can be obtained via the method `getStatus()`.)

If the thread is ready, then it must be removed from the ready queue. If a running thread is being destroyed, then it must be removed from controlling the CPU, as described earlier.

There is nothing special to do if the killed thread has status `ThreadWaiting` (at any level). However, you are not done yet. First, the thread being destroyed might have initiated an I/O operation and thus is suspended on the corresponding IORB. The I/O request might have been enqueued to some device and has not been processed because the device may be busy with other work. What should now happen to the IORB? Should you just let the device work on a request that came from a dead thread?

The answer is that you should cancel the I/O request by removing the corresponding IORB from its device queue. This can be done by scanning all devices in the device table and executing the method `cancelPendingIO()` on each device. The device table is an array of size `Device.getTableSize()` (starting with device 0), where device `i` can be obtained with a call to `Device.get()`.

During the run, threads may acquire and release shared resources that are needed for the execution. Therefore, when a thread is killed, those resources must be released into the common pool so that other threads could use them. This is done using the static method `giveupResources()` of class `Resource-CB`, which accepts the thread be killed as a parameter.

Two things remain to be done now. First, you must dispatch a new thread, since you should use every interrupt or a system call as an opportunity to optimize CPU usage. Second, since you have just killed a thread, you must check if the corresponding task still has any threads left. A task with no threads is considered dead and must be destroyed with the `kill()` method of class `TaskCB`. To find out the number of threads a task has, use the method `getThreadCount()` of `TaskCB`.

◇ `public void do_suspend(Event event)`
   To suspend a thread, you must first figure out which state to suspend it to. As can be seen from Figure 4.2, there are two candidates: If the thread is running, then it is suspended to `ThreadWaiting`. If it is already waiting, then the status is incremented by 1. For instance, if the current status of the thread is `ThreadWaiting` then it should become `ThreadWaiting+1`. You now must set the new thread status using the method `setStatus()` and place it on the waiting queue to the event.

If `suspend()` is called to suspend the running thread, then the thread must lose control of the CPU. Switching control of the CPU can also be done in the dispatcher (as part of the context switch), but it has to be done somewhere to avert an error.

Finally, a new thread must be dispatched using a call to `dispatch()`.

◇ `public void do_resume()`
   A waiting thread can be resumed to a waiting state at a lower level (e.g., `ThreadWaiting+2` to `ThreadWaiting+1` to `ThreadWaiting` or from `ThreadWaiting` to the status `ThreadReady`). If the thread becomes ready, it should be placed on the ready queue for future scheduling. Finally, a new thread should be dispatched.

Note that there is no need to take the resumed thread out of the waiting queue to any event. A typical sequence of actions that leads to a call to `resume()` is as follows: When an event happens, the method `notifyThreads()` is invoked on the appropriate `Event` object. This method examines the waiting queue of the event, removes the threads blocked on this event one by one, and calls `resume()` on each such thread. So, by the time `do_resume()` is called, the corresponding thread is no longer on the waiting queue of the event.

◇ `public static int do_dispatch()`

This method is where thread scheduling takes place. Scheduling can be as simple as plain round-robin or as complex as multi-queue scheduling with feedback. $\mathcal{OSP}$ 2 does not impose any restrictions on how scheduling is to be done, provided that the following conventions are followed.

First, some thread should be chosen from the ready queue (or the currently running thread can be allowed to continue). If a new thread is chosen, *context switch* must be performed, as described earlier, and `SUCCESS` returned. If no ready-to-run thread can be found, `FAILURE` must be returned.

Relevant methods defined in other packages.   Apart from the methods of the `Event` class listed above, the following methods of other classes should or can be used to implement the methods in class `ThreadCB` as described above:

◇ `final public int getDeviceID()`   IORB
   Returns the device Id number that this I/O request is for.

◇ `final static public Device getDevice(int deviceID)`   Device
   Returns the device object corresponding to the given Id number.

◇ `final static public int getTableSize()`   Device
   Tells how many devices there are. The number is specified in the parameter file and can vary from one simulation run to another.

◇ `final static public Device get(int deviceID)`   Device
   Returns the device object with the given Id. In conjunction with `getTableSize()`, this method can be used in a loop to examine each device in turn. Note that all devices are mounted by $\mathcal{OSP}$ 2 at the beginning of the simulation and no devices are added or removed during a simulation run. Therefore the number of devices remains constant and the device table has no "holes".

⋄ `public void cancelPendingIO(ThreadCB th)`   Device
The context for this method is a device object, and the method cancels pending IORBs of the thread *th* on that device. This is done when *th* is killed to prevent the servicing of pending I/O's requested by killed threads. However, this method does not cancel the IORB that is currently being serviced by the device. The device is just allowed to finish.

⋄ `final static public PageTable getPTBR()`   MMU
This method returns the value of the page table base register (PTBR) of the MMU. PTBR holds a reference to the page table of the currently running task.

⋄ `static public void setPTBR(PageTable table)`   MMU
This method allows one to set the value of PTBR. When no thread is running, the value should be null; otherwise, it must be the page table of the task that owns the currently running thread.

⋄ `public final TaskCB getTask()`   PageTable
Returns the task that owns the page table.

⋄ `public void kill()`   TaskCB
Kills the task on which this method is invoked.

⋄ `public int getThreadCount()`   TaskCB
Tells how many threads the task has.

⋄ `public int addThread(ThreadCB thread)`   TaskCB
Attaches a newly created thread to task. Returns SUCCESS or FAILURE.

⋄ `public int removeThread(ThreadCB thread)`   TaskCB
Removes killed thread to task.

⋄ `public ThreadCB getCurrentThread()`   TaskCB
Returns the current thread object of the task.

⋄ `public void setCurrentThread(ThreadCB t)`   TaskCB
Sets the current thread of the task to the given thread.

⋄ `final public int getPriority()`   TaskCB
Tells the priority of the task.

⋄ `final public void setPriority(int p)`   TaskCB
Sets the priority of the task. The `setPriority()`/`getPriority()` methods are provided for convenience, in case priority scheduling is used and dispatching takes into account the priority of both the task and the thread.

⋄ `final public PageTable getPageTable()`   TaskCB
Returns the page table of the task.

◇ `final public int getStatus()`   TaskCB
   Returns the task's status.

◇ `set()` and `get()`   HTimer
   These classes can be used to set and query the hardware timer. See Section 1.4 for details.

◇ `get()`   HClock
   This method is described in Section 1.4; it is used to query the hardware clock of the simulated machine.

◇ `public static void giveupResources(ThreadCB thread)`   ResourceCB
   Releases all abstract shared resources held by the thread. Note: these resources do not include concrete resources such as memory or CPU.

Summary of Class `ThreadCB`

The following table summarizes the attributes of class `ThreadCB` and the methods for manipulating them. These attributes and methods are provided by the class `IflThreadCB` and are inherited. The methods appearing in the table are more fully described in Section 4.5.

Task: The task that owns the thread. This property can be set and queried via the methods `setTask()` and `getTask()`.

Identity: The identity of a thread can be obtained using the method `getID()`. This property is set by the system.

Status: The status of the thread. The relevant methods are `setStatus()` and `getStatus()`.

Priority: The priority of the thread. The methods to query and change thread's priority are `setPriority()` and `getPriority()`.

Creation time: The value of this property can be obtained using the method `getCreationTime()`.

CPU time used: The total CPU time used by the thread can be obtained via the method `getTimeOnCPU()`.

4.4 The Class `TimerInterruptHandler`

This class is much simpler than `ThreadCB`. It is defined as `public class TimerInterruptHandler extends IflTimerInterruptHandler`

and contains only one method:

⋄ `public void do_handleInterrupt()`
This method is called by the general interrupt handler when the system
timer expires. The timer interrupt handler is the simplest of all interrupt
handlers in $\mathcal{OSP}$ 2. Its main purpose is to schedule the next thread to run
and, possibly, to set the timer to cause an interrupt again after a certain
time interval. Resetting the times can also be done in the `dispatch()`
method of `ThreadCB` instead, because the dispatcher might want to have
full control over CPU time slices allocated to threads.

Relevant methods defined in other packages.   The following is a list
of methods that belong to other classes and might be useful for implementing
`do_handleInterrupt()`:

⋄ `final static public void set(int time)`   HTimer
Sets the hardware timer to `time` ticks from now. Cancels the previously set
timer, if any.

⋄ `final static public int get()`   HTimer
Returns the time left to the next timer interrupt.

4.5 Methods Exported by the THREADS Package

The following is a summary of the public methods defined in the classes of the
THREADS package or in the corresponding superclasses, which can be used to
implement this and other student packages. To the right of each method we
list the class of the objects to which the method applies. In the case of the
THREADS package, all exported methods belong to the class `TaskCB`, which
inherits them from the superclass `IflTaskCB`.

⋄ `final public static ThreadCB create()`   ThreadCB
This method is a wrapper around the method `do_create()` described in
this chapter. It is provided by `IflThreadCB` and is inherited by `ThreadCB`.
Returns the created thread.

⋄ `final public static void dispatch()`   ThreadCB
This is a wrapper around the method `do_dispatch()` described in this
chapter. This method is provided by `IflThreadCB` and is inherited by
`ThreadCB`.

⋄ `final public void suspend(Event event)`   ThreadCB
This is a wrapper around the method `do_suspend()` described in this chapter. This method is provided by `IflThreadCB` and is inherited by `ThreadCB`.

⋄ `final public void resume()` ThreadCB
   This is a wrapper around the method `do_resume()` described in this chapter. This method is defined in `IflThreadCB`, but it is inherited by `ThreadCB`.

⋄ `final public void kill()` ThreadCB
   This is a wrapper around the method `do_kill()` described in this chapter. This method is defined in `IflThreadCB`, but it is inherited by `ThreadCB`.

⋄ `final public TaskCB getTask()` ThreadCB
   Returns the task this thread belongs to.

⋄ `final public void setTask(TaskCB t)` ThreadCB
   Sets the task of the thread.

⋄ `final public int getStatus()` ThreadCB
   Returns the status of this thread.

⋄ `final public void setStatus(int s)` ThreadCB
   Sets the status of this thread.

⋄ `public double getTimeOnCPU()` ThreadCB
   Tells the total time the thread has been using CPU.

⋄ `final public long getCreationTime()` ThreadCB
   Returns the creation time of the thread.

⋄ `final public int getPriority()` ThreadCB
   Tells the priority of this thread.

⋄ `final public void setPriority(int p)` ThreadCB
   Sets the priority. The `setPriority` and `getPriority` methods are provided for convenience, in case the assignment calls for priority scheduling. *OSP 2* does not actually care how priority is used, if at all.

5
MEMORY: *Virtual Memory Management*

5.1 Chapter Objective

The objective of project MEMORY is to teach students about virtual memory and other modern memory-management techniques and to provide them with a well-structured programming environment in which to implement these techniques. To this end, students will be asked to implement the five public classes of the MEMORY package. The main class, MMU, represents the memory-management unit, the piece of hardware that is responsible for memory access in a computer. The other classes are FrameTableEntry, PageFaultHandler, PageTableEntry, and PageTable. All of these classes are described in detail later on in the chapter, each in its own subsection. We begin with an overview of memory-management basics.

5.2 Overview of Memory Management

In a modern computer, the portion of the circuitry called the **memory management unit** (abbr. MMU) is responsible for providing access to main memory. In *OSP 2*, memory access is simulated by calling the method refer() of the class MMU, which is one of the key methods to be implemented in this project. It may seem strange at first that you are being asked to implement a piece of hardware as part of an operating systems programming project. However, the

MMU is the gateway to memory for executing threads, and it provides you with a golden opportunity to implement the memory-management technique your MEMORY assignment calls for.

Memory management and multiprogramming.   Modern memory-management techniques are aimed at supporting multiprogramming and must therefore allow multiple processes or threads to be memory-resident simultaneously. In this way, when the currently executed thread becomes blocked, e.g. waiting for an I/O request to complete, control of the CPU can be easily switched to another memory-resident thread, albeit one that is in the ready state waiting to resume execution.

Partitioning memory.   The basic memory-management technique in support of multiprogramming is to partition main memory into, shall we say, partitions or chunks of memory that different processes can occupy. Partitions can be either fixed-size or variable-size. The former results in internal fragmentation, which occurs when a process does not utilize the entirety of a partition. The latter results in external fragmentation, which occurs when a partition is too small to be of use to any process. We shall focus the remainder of our overview of memory-management basics on the fixed-sized partitions utilized by a technique known as paging. Segmentation is an alternative to paging that uses variable-size partitions.

Logical memory.   The big advance in memory management came with the realization that the memory allocated to a process need not be contiguous! In the case of paging, a partition is called a page and a process's pages collectively make up its logical address space. Physical memory is divided into page frames, each the size of a page so the fit of a page in a page frame is exact. Thus, in theory, a page of a process can be placed in any available page frame. The point is that the pages of a process's logical address space may be dispersed noncontiguously among the page frames of main memory. Page sizes typically range from 512 bytes to 4K bytes but whatever the page size, it is fixed throughout system execution.

The primary mechanisms used for implementing logical memory are the **page table base register** (abbr. PTBR) and the **page table**. The key issue here is logical address translation, how to convert a logical address into a physical address, and this is the responsibility of the MMU. A logical address is just string of bits (e.g. 32 in the case of a 32-bit machine architecture) that can be logically viewed as consisting of two parts: a page number and a byte offset into the page. The number of bits taken up by the first part will depend on the page size: 9 for a page size of 512 bytes, 10 for a page size of 1K bytes, etc. The remainder of the address bits are interpreted as the byte offset into the logical page being addressed.

Every process has a page table of its own and when a thread is dispatched on the CPU, the address of the page table of the process to which the thread belongs is placed in the PTBR. The MMU uses the PTBR to find the location of the page table and uses the page table to supply the mapping between the logical memory of processes and the main memory of the computer, represented by the physical page frames. The overall schema is depicted in Figure 5.1.

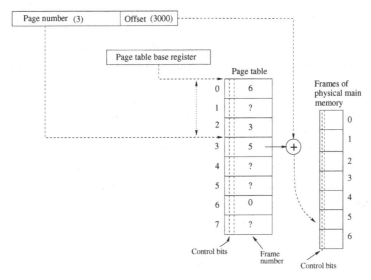

Figure 5.1 Logical/Virtual address translation using page tables.

Virtual memory. The simple memory-addressing mechanism just described works well as long as the frames corresponding to the pages of a process are all in main memory. However, as seen in Figure 5.1, some entries in a page table do not necessarily have to have frames assigned to them. The key insight behind virtual memory is that a page table can have more entries than the number of physical page frames, so a one-to-one assignment of frames to pages might not be possible. In other words, the size of virtual memory can and normally does exceed that of physical memory. Note that we use the term virtual memory now instead of logical memory to emphasize the fact that larger-than-physical-memory address spaces are supported by this scheme.

Pagefaults.   The key mechanism for implementing virtual memory is that each page table entry has a **validity bit**, which indicates whether the page has a main-memory frame assigned to it. This bit is checked by the MMU hardware and whenever a running thread makes a reference to a page whose validity bit is zero, a **pagefault** occurs: a special kind of interrupt that is used to notify the operating system of references to frame-less pages. The intended response from the OS is to assign a suitable frame to the page. The module responsible for this action is called the **pagefault handler**. A page whose validity bit is one (i.e. has a page frame assigned to it) is said to be *valid*.

Before examing the steps involved in handling a pagefault, let us first look more carefully at frame-less pages and their relationship to other resources owned by processes. If no frame is assigned to a page, where is the program code or data that the running thread is supposedly referencing? The answer is that a copy of the entire process space is kept in secondary storage on a **swap device**. In high-performance systems, a swap device can be a separate disk, but typically it is just a partition occupying part of a physical disk. Nevertheless, the operating system assigns a **logical device** to each such partition and at that level the swap device can be viewed as a separate device with its own characteristics and device number. In particular, in $\mathcal{OSP}$ *2*, a swap device is viewed as a real device with a special device number, `SwapDeviceID`. Thus, every process (i.e., OSP task) has a corresponding **swap file** on the swap device, which contains an exact image of the process memory.

When a pagefault on page P of task T occurs, the pagefault handler has to do several things:

1. Suspend the thread that caused the interrupt until the situation that gave rise to the pagefault is rectified. This is done by creating a *new* event, `pfEvent`, of type `SystemEvent` and then executing `suspend()` on the thread using `pfEvent` as a parameter. A new system event is created using the constructor `SystemEvent()` of class `SystemEvent`. This event must be kept around until the end of pagefault processing, as it is needed to resume the thread before returning from the pagefault handler.

2. Find a suitable frame to assign to page P.
   An obvious choice would be a free frame, i.e., a frame that is not assigned to any other page (of this or any other task). But there might not be such a frame at the moment (remember that there are fewer frames than pages!). In this case, **page replacement** must be performed, as described below. The result of a successful page-replacement action is that a free frame becomes available and is assigned to page P.

3. Perform a *swap-in*.
   Once a frame is assigned to the faulty page, you need to make sure that it

contains the exact image of the page, which is available in the task's swap file. To do this, the pagefault handler must initiate a *swap-in*: a file read operation that would input the requisite page from the swap device and store it in the frame.

4. Suspend the pagefault handler.
   An I/O operation takes time, so the pagefault handler must suspend itself until it is woken up by the disk interrupt coming from the swap device.[1] Suspension of the pagefault handler actually happens as part of the file read operation that swaps the page in—you do not need to do this explicitly.

5. Finish up.
   Once the image of the right page is copied into the frame, the pagefault handler should update the page table to make sure that the page entry is pointing to the right frame, and set the validity bit of the page appropriately. Next, the thread that caused the pagefault should be resumed and placed on the queue of the ready-to-run threads. This is done by executing the method `notifyThreads()` on the event `pfEvent`, which was created in Step 1. Finally, as with any other interrupt handler, the dispatcher should be called to give control of the CPU to some ready-to-run thread.

Page replacement. In describing the actions of the pagefault handler, we deliberately omitted a saga of its own: What should you do if, in Step 2, the pagefault handler cannot find a free frame? In this case, it becomes necessary to choose a frame F' occupied by some other page P' and use F' to satisfy the pagefault. The page P' is often called a **victim page** and it is said that the pagefault handler *evicts* this page from its frame.

The algorithm deployed by the pagefault handler for choosing such a frame is called the page-replacement algorithm, and the most well-known algorithm of this kind is LRU (Least Recently Used). LRU replaces the page in memory that has not been referenced for the longest time. Assuming that threads exhibit the principle of locality, meaning that they cluster memory references around a certain subset of their pages over a given window of time, then the LRU page should be the least likely page to be referenced in the near future and its replacement is a good bet.

The problem with the LRU policy is that it can be difficult to implement and for this reason other algorithms have been developed to approximate the performance of LRU while imposing little overhead. Many of these algorithms

---

[1] Handling disk interrupts is part of another project, module DEVICES. In the present project, one should assume that the disk interrupt handler functions according to the specifications given below.

are variants of a scheme known as the **clock policy**, which associates one or more **use bits** with each frame and organizes the frames as a circular buffer. Consider for simplicity the case of a single use bit added to each frame. A frame's use bit is set to 1 when a page is first loaded in the frame and whenever the page in the frame is referenced. When it comes time to replace a page, the clock algorithm scans the buffer looking for a frame with a use bit of zero; the page occupying the first such frame is chosen for replacement. Each time it encounters a frame with a use bit of 1, it resets that bit to zero and moves on to the next frame in the buffer. The use of multiple use bits per frame increases the algorithm's precision: the more use bits per frame deployed, the more closely the algorithm is able to approximate LRU.

From a performance perspective, a good page-replacement algorithm is characterized by a low pagefault rate. However, as far as the operating system is concerned, the only requirement of a page-replacement algorithm is that there should be no "undesirable side effects". One such side effect is due to the nature of the I/O subsystem. Suppose that a page-replacement algorithm chooses a frame F' that is involved in an active I/O operation. In some cases, a device that started an I/O cannot be stopped. So if you reuse the corresponding frame for some other purpose then the data in the frame may become corrupted (in case of a file-read operation) or, in case of a write operation, the data being written out might become corrupted if you change the content of the frame before the I/O is finished. Even if the device can be stopped immediately, it might still not be a good idea because stopping the device now might mean that the same I/O operation would have to be re-issued later.

Locking and unlocking of frames.   How can an OS protect the frames associated with active I/O operations? A typical mechanism is to keep, for each frame, a count of the active or outstanding I/O operations that involve that frame. There are a variety of ways to maintain such a count. Here is an explanation of how it is done in *OSP 2*. When an I/O operation is to be performed on a certain I/O device, an I/O request block (abbr. IORB) is enqueued on the device's device queue. An IORB does not refer to frames directly. Instead, it references the *page* that is involved in the I/O. The thread that requested the I/O must perform a `lock()` operation (which is a method of class `PageTable-Entry`) on the page involved. If no frame is assigned to the page, a pagefault occurs, and the IORB will not be enqueued on the device until the pagefault processing is over. The `lock()` operation increments the **lock count** of the frame associated with the page and the `unlock()` operation decrements it. A page is considered to be locked in a frame if the lock count of the associated frame is a positive number.

Thus, by the time the IORB makes it to the device queue, the page involved is locked and has an associated frame. The page-replacement mechanism is prohibited from taking frames that have positive lock counts.

Note that a page involved in an I/O is locked into a frame when the corresponding IORB is *enqueued* on the device queue of the device in question (a device might be busy and have a queue of outstanding I/O's), not when the IORB is selected for processing by the device. The reason should be obvious: To perform an I/O, the page referenced by the IORB must be in some frame in main memory. If not, it would have to be swapped in. But this requires another I/O and takes time. So, the selected IORB cannot be processed and the device would remain idle. In contrast, if pages are locked just before the IORB is enqueued, the corresponding frames would remain protected for the entire period while the IORB remains on the device queue (and until the device finishes the corresponding I/O). If the page being locked is frame-less, a pagefault occurs and the page is brought in *before* the IORB is selected for processing.

Dirty frames.   Locking is not the only constraint that a page-replacement mechanism must abide by. Another issue has to do with so-called **dirty frames**. A dirty frame is one whose contents has been changed since the last time a page was swapped into the frame. If such a frame is chosen for replacement, the current contents of the frame must be saved in the swap file of the task that owns the page that currently occupies the frame. Otherwise, all changes made to the page will be lost. Thus, each frame needs another bit, the **dirty bit**, which indicates whether the contents of the frame has been changed. The actions that change the contents of a frame are the memory operation (`MemoryWrite`) and the I/O operation `read()`, which transfers data from a file to main memory.

Thus, we see that finding a victim page and evicting it is no simple matter: It may require an extra I/O operation to *swap-out* the victim page and synchronize its contents with the contents of that page in the swap file.

Frame table.   Information about physical, main-memory frames is kept in the **frame table**: an array that has one entry per frame. Each entry is an object of the class `FrameTableEntry`. In fact, an $\mathcal{OSP}\ 2$ frame table contains more information than that. For instance, each frame entry contains a back reference to the page that occupies that frame (or `null`). Every frame entry also has a so-called **reference bit**, which indicates whether the frame has been *referenced* (as the result of executing `refer()` or due to I/O into or out of the frame). The reference bit often plays a role (as a use bit) in page-replacement algorithms.

In real computers, the reference and dirty bits are set in hardware but they are unset by software using special instructions. In contrast the lock count and

the page reference in the frame table are manipulated entirely in software. In
OSP 2 you have to set and unset all of these items in software. In this sense, part
of what you will do to implement the `refer()` method is really a simulation of
various hardware functions. This includes setting the dirty and the reference
bits, and also causing the pagefault interrupt itself. We describe these issues in
more detail in Section 5.6.

Reserved frames.   In OSP 2, frames have yet another bit, the **reserved
bit**. Like the lock count, a reserved bit protects frames from the page-
replacement mechanism, but it is used for a different reason. Suppose a thread
Th causes a pagefault on page P and control is transferred to the pagefault handler after blocking Th. The pagefault handler may go through several distinct
phases:

1. Finding a suitable frame F. Suppose F is dirty and is currently occupied
   by page P'.

2. Evicting P' by issuing an I/O operation that swaps P' out.

3. Waiting for the I/O to finish.

4. Initiating an I/O to swap page P into frame F.

5. Waiting for the I/O to finish.

6. Putting Th on the ready queue and quitting.

The problem is that while locking will prevent F from being grabbed by other
threads *during* phases 3 and 5, nothing prevents it from being grabbed to
satisfy other pagefaults between phases 1 and 2, between phases 3 and 5, and
after phase 5. Thus, it might well happen that after trying so hard to assign a
suitable frame to page P, the pagefault handler will find the frame stolen from
under its nose before it gets a chance to assign F to P. To prevent this kind of
unproductive behavior, the pagefault handler must *reserve* frame F in phase 1
and *un-reserve* it in phase 6.

Prepaging.   Some pagefault handling algorithms perform **prepaging**, i.e.,
the swapping in of invalid pages that *did not* cause the pagefault. These algorithms are trying to guess which pages might be referenced by the thread
in the near future and swap them in proactively. To implement prepaging, the
pagefault handler can issue additional `read()` operations, which might require
`write()` operations to swap some other pages out.

   Prepaging a page is similar to bringing a page in as part of regular pagefault processing. However, selecting a frame for prepaging should be done with

caution. In particular, make sure that it is not the frame that was selected for the original faulty page. Otherwise, you will end up evicting the page that the pagefault handler was supposed to make valid!

Since prepaging involves I/O, it is possible that the thread that initiated the pagefault will be killed by the time prepaging is finished. When this happens, prepaging should stop. One special case arises when prepaging is done from within the pagefault handler. The question then is what should be the return code for do_handlePageFault(): SUCCESS or FAILURE? $\mathcal{OSP}$ 2 expects FAILURE in this case. In particular, if the page that caused the pagefault became valid before the thread was killed, the page should be made invalid again prior to returning from the pagefault handler. However, you should realize that a more optimized operating system might make a different decision and keep such a page valid, because it might be used by other threads of the same task.

Proactive page cleaning.   Some memory-management algorithms perform proactive page cleaning by periodically swapping them out on disk (but not invalidating them). The idea is to utilize the times when the swap device is idle and reduce the time needed to handle pagefaults by increasing the supply of clean pages.

Technically, this is done by setting up **daemons**: special system threads that are set to wake up periodically, perform the job assigned to them, and go back to sleep. We discussed the $\mathcal{OSP}$ 2 support for daemons in Section 1.7.

In order to set up a cleaning daemon, one creates a class that implements **DaemonInterface** (see Section 1.7). The required method **unleash()** can then be made to execute the proactive cleaning algorithm. An essential part of this algorithm is a series of **write()** operations that write dirty frames out to the swap device (but keeps these pages valid). This daemon must be registered with the system at startup, as explained in Section 1.7.

Having surveyed the major issues involved in pagefault handling, we are now ready to discuss the actual $\mathcal{OSP}$ 2 classes and methods that constitute the MEMORY module. The class diagrams of Figure 5.2 and Figure 5.3 place these classes in a larger context.

5.3 Class FrameTableEntry

This class implements the entries in the frame table, the main repository of information about the status of the main-memory frames. It is defined as follows:

◇ public class FrameTableEntry extends IflFrameTableEntry

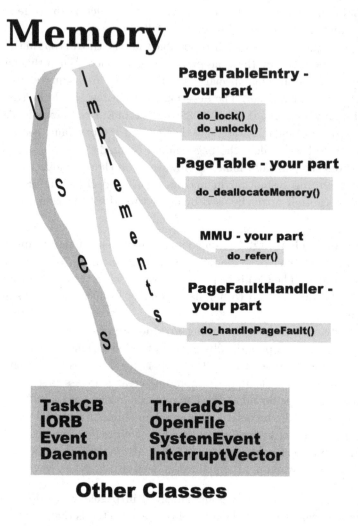

Figure 5.2 Overview of the package MEMORY, I.

The class constructor is the only method of this class that needs to be implemented as part of the project:

◇ public FrameTableEntry(int frameID)
  Calls super(frameID) and might perform other initializations if the student implementation defines additional fields in this class.

Memory

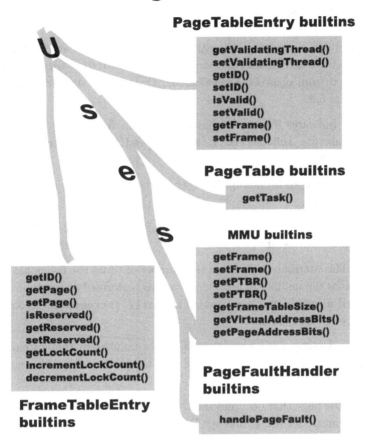

Figure 5.3 Overview of the package MEMORY, II.

However, this class inherits a number of methods from its superclasses, and these methods are used by other classes in this project:

◇ `public final int getLockCount()`
  Returns the lock count of the frame.

◇ `final public void incrementLockCount()`
  Increments the lock count of the frame by 1.

◇ `final public void decrementLockCount()`
   Decrements the lock count of the frame by 1.

Summary of Class `FrameTableEntry`

The following table summarizes the attributes of the class `FrameTableEntry` and the methods for setting and querying them. These attributes and methods are all inherited from class `IflFrameTableEntry` and are described in more detail in Section 5.8.

Reserved flag: Indicates if a thread has reserved this frame. The corresponding methods are `isReserved()`, `getReserved()`, `setReserved()`, and `setUnreserved()`.

Dirty flag: The methods for manipulating the dirtiness of a frame are `isDirty()` and `setDirty()`.

Reference flag: Indicates if the frame has been referenced. The methods that handle this attribute are `getreferenced()` and `setreferenced()`.

Lock count: This attribute represents the number of times the frame has been locked minus the number of unlock operations performed on the frame, and is accessed using the methods `getLockCount()`, `incrementLockCount()`, and `decrementLockCount()`.

Identity: The identity of a frame is its sequence number in the system-wide array of all main-memory frames. It can be queried using the method `getID()`.

Page: This is the page that occupies the frame (null, if the frame is free). This attribute can be set using `setPage()` and retrieved using `getPage()`.

It should be noted that some information (such as page information and identity) in the $\mathcal{OSP}$ 2 frame table entries is redundant and is not present in the frame table of a typical operating system. In fact, the $\mathcal{OSP}$ 2 frame table can be seen as a cross between a normal frame table and what is known as an **inverted page table**.

5.4 Class `PageTableEntry`

This class implements the data structure that describes each entry in the page table. It is defined as follows:

⋄ public class PageTableEntry extends IflPageTableEntry

For this project, the student must implement the following methods of this class:

⋄ public int do_lock(IORB iorb)

The ultimate goal of this method is to increment the lock count of the frame associated with the page. However, the details are not as simple as one might think, because the page might be invalid at the time the lock operation is performed.

Thus, this method must first check if the page is in main memory by testing the validity bit of the page (using the method isValid()). If the page is invalid, a pagefault must be initiated.

To initiate a pagefault, the do_lock() method calls the static method handlePageFault() of class PageFaultHandler, i.e., it calls the pagefault handler directly, without initiating an interrupt. Note that page locking is performed as part of an I/O request, when the CPU is already in kernel mode, so there is no need to cause an interrupt.

We have already seen that page locking involves considerably more than simply incrementing the lock count. Yet, there is still much more to do. Consider the following situation. Suppose thread Th_1 of task T makes a reference to page P either via the refer() operation or through locking. If the page is invalid, a pagefault is initiated. Suppose now that thread Th_2 of the same task comes along and also wants to lock the same page P. Should this cause a pagefault as well? The answer, of course, is no. The pagefault handler must already have found a suitable frame for P and the corresponding I/O requests must already be in the pipeline. Another pagefault would only confuse the system.

To help identify the pages that are involved in a pagefault, $\mathcal{OSP}$ 2 provides the method getValidatingThread(). When applied to a page, this method returns the thread that caused a pagefault on that page (or null, if the page is not involved in a pagefault). In our case, this method would return Th_1.

The proper action for Th_2 depends on whether $Th_2 = Th_1$. If $Th_2 = Th_1$, then the proper action is to return right after incrementing the lock count.[2]

---

[2] You might be wondering how a thread that caused a pagefault can come back and request a lock on the page. The answer is simple: The lock can be requested by the swap-in I/O operation that must be performed as part of pagefault handling. This swap-in operation is performed on behalf of the same thread that caused the pagefault, so the locking thread and the validating thread would be one and the same.

If $Th_2 \neq Th_1$, then the proper action is to wait until P becomes valid. This is easy to accomplish because the class PageTableEntry happens to be a subclass of Event (see Section 4.3 for the description of this class). Thus, we can execute the suspend() method on Th_2 and pass page P as a parameter.

When the page becomes valid (or if the pagefault handler fails to make the page valid, say, because the original thread, Th_1, that caused the pagefault was killed during the wait), the threads waiting on the page will be unblocked by the pagefault handler (which is another class in this project) and will be able to continue. When such threads become unblocked inside the do_lock() method, control falls through the call to suspend() and the do_lock() method must exit and return the appropriate value: SUCCESS if the page became valid as a result of the pagefault and FAILURE otherwise.

In general, do_lock() returns SUCCESS if the page was locked successfully (which does not necessarily involve a pagefault) or FAILURE if the page was not locked. The latter can happen if either the pagefault (which might occur due to locking) fails or if the thread that created iorb was killed while waiting for the lock operation to complete.

Finally, in the case of a successful return, you should remember to increment the lock count of the frame associated with the page, i.e., to do the actual locking. (Note that the focus of the previous discussion was on ensuring that the page is associated with a frame.) Incrementing the lock count of a frame is accomplished using method incrementLockCount() of class FrameTable-Entry.

⋄ public void do_unlock()
Unlocking is, fortunately, much simpler than locking. All that is needed is to decrement the lock count via a call to decrementLockCount() of class FrameTableEntry. Make sure that the lock count does not become negative, which is a sign of a problem.

Relevant methods defined in other classes.   The following is a list of methods from other classes that can be useful in implementing the methods of class PageTableEntry:

⋄ public final int getLockCount()   FrameTableEntry
  Returns the lock count of the frame.

⋄ final public void incrementLockCount()   FrameTableEntry
  Increments the lock count of the frame by 1.

⋄ final public void decrementLockCount()   FrameTableEntry
  Decrements the lock count of the frame by 1.

⋄ `final public ThreadCB getValidatingThread()`   `PageTableEntry`
Returns the validating thread of the page, i.e., the thread that caused
the pagefault on this page. If the page is not in pagefault or its validating
thread was killed before the page became valid, then this method returns
`null`.
This method is inherited from a superclasses of `PageTableEntry`.

⋄ `final public void suspend(Event event)`   `ThreadCB`
Suspends the thread on which this method is called and puts the thread
on the waiting queue of `event`.

⋄ `final public int getStatus()`   `TaskCB`
Returns the task's status.

⋄ `final public int getStatus()`   `ThreadCB`
Returns the status of this thread.

⋄ `public final boolean isValid()`   `PageTableEntry`
Tells if the page is valid by checking the validity bit.

⋄ `public final boolean isReserved()`   `FrameTableEntry`
Tests if the frame is reserved.

⋄ `public final ThreadCB getThread()`   `IORB`
Returns the thread that requested the I/O.

⋄ `final public int getDeviceID()`   `IORB`
Returns the device involved in the I/O operation.

⋄ `final public int getIOType()`   `IORB`
Returns the I/O type represented by the IORB. $\mathcal{OSP}$ 2 supports two types:
`FileRead` and `FileWrite`.

Summary of Class `PageTableEntry`

The following is a summary of the main attributes of class `PageTableEntry`
and the methods for manipulating them. See Section 5.8 for a description of
these methods.

Validity flag: The validity flag is handled by the methods `isValid()` and
`setValid()`.

Frame: If the page is valid, there must be a frame associated with it, which
is described by this attribute. The corresponding methods are `getFrame()`
and `setFrame()`.

Identity: The identity of a page is its sequence number in the corresponding page table. It is set automatically by the system and can be queried using getID().

Owner task: Points to the task that owns the page and is queried using method getTask() of PageTableEntry. This attribute is not really stored with the page; it is rather an attribute of the table to which the page belongs. Thus, this method simply queries the corresponding attribute of the page table.

Validating thread: If the page is currently in pagefault processing, this is the thread that caused the pagefault. This thread can be obtained using the method getValidatingThread() and is set using setValidatingThread().

5.5 Class PageTable

The class PageTable represents page tables and is defined as follows:

◇ public class PageTable extends IflPageTable

The only mandatory method to be implemented here is the class constructor:

◇ public PageTable(TaskCB ownerTask)
This constructor gets as a parameter the task for which the table is to be created. It first calls super(ownerTask), as all *OSP 2* constructors must do, and then constructs the page table. The page table is assumed to be an array of size equal to the maximum number of pages allowed, and is accessible through the variable pages inherited from the superclass Ifl-PageTable. The maximal number of pages allowed is calculated using the method MMU.getPageAddressBits(), which represents the number of bits dedicated to representing a page number out of the total number of bits in an address.

After calling super(), the variable pages must be initialized to a new array of PageTableEntry whose size is determined as described above. Then each page must be initialized with a suitable PageTableEntry object using the constructor of that class. Make sure that you use correct page id numbers and the correct page table in the PageTableEntry constructor when creating these page objects.

◇ public void do_deallocateMemory()
This method is typically invoked by a terminating task on its page table object to unset the various flags for the frames allocated to the task. Specifically, it uses setPage() to nullify the page field that points to the page that occupies the frame (thereby freeing the frame), setDirty() to clean the page,

and `setReferenced()` to unset the reference bit. It also un-reserves each frame that was reserved by that task. To find out which task has reserved a given frame, use the method `getReserved()` of class `FrameTableEntry`.

Note that this method does not need to (and should not) set the frame attribute of the deallocated pages to null. It is possible that some of these pages are being used by ongoing I/O operations that pump data into or out of the frames that are currently allocated to the killed task. The disk interrupt handler (which will be called each time an I/O is finished) needs to know both the frame and the page objects involved in the finished operation, and it gets the former from the latter.

Note that if a page of a killed task is locked, it can be unlocked only by the device interrupt handler. Unlocking inside the memory-management module can lead to inconsistencies. Try to analyze what might happen in this case in order to understand why this is dangerous.

Summary of Class `PageTable`

Here is a summary of the attributes and methods of class `PageTable`. All of these attributes are provided by class `IflPageTable` and are inherited from there.

Page table: This is an array referenced by the variable `pages`. This array is created in the `PageTable()` constructor.

Owner task: Describes the task to which the page table belongs, which can be obtained via the method `getTask()`.

5.6 Class MMU

This class represents the memory-management unit of the simulated computer, and defines three methods: the initialization method that exist in every student module and `do_refer()`, which represents memory references made by the CPU while executing computer instructions. A detailed explanation is given below.

⋄ `public static void init()`
This method is called once, at the beginning, to initialize the data structures. Typically, it is used to initialize the frame table.

Since the total number of frames is known (`MMU.getFrameTableSize()`), each frame in the frame table can be initialized in a `for`-loop. Initially, all entries in the frame table are just null-objects and must be set to real frame table objects using the FrameTableEntry() constructor. To set a frame entry, use the method setFrame() in class MMU.

Another use of the init() method is for the initialization of private static variables defined in other classes of the MEMORY package. For example, one can define an init() method in class PageFaultHandler which would be able to access any variable defined in that class. Then MMU.init() can call PageFaultHandler.init(). Since MMU.init() is called at the very beginning of the simulation, PageFaultHandler.init() is also going to be called at the beginning of the simulation.

◇ public PageTableEntry do_refer(int memoryAddress,
int referenceType,ThreadCB thread)
   This method takes an address of a byte in the logical memory of the thread, a type of the memory reference (MemoryRead, MemoryWrite, or MemoryLock) and a thread that made the reference. The method then needs to determine the page of the thread's logical memory to which the reference was made. The methods getVirtualAddressBits() and getPageAddressBits(), both inherited from the superclass If1MMU, can be used to determine the number of bits allocated to represent the offset within the page. This number can then be used to compute the page size and then the page to which memoryAddress belongs.

Next, the method must check if the page is valid (the method isValid()). If so, you only need to appropriately set the referenced and the dirty bits of the page, and quit.

If the page is invalid, things are more interesting. There are two possibilities:

1. Some other thread of the same task has already caused a pagefault and the page is already on its way to main memory.

2. No other thread caused a pagefault on this invalid page.

As before, you can tell one case from the other with the help of the method getValidatingThread().

In the first case, the thread (that was passed as a parameter to do_refer()) should simply suspend itself on the page and wait until the page becomes valid. When the page eventually becomes valid, the method should set the referenced and dirty bits appropriately and quit. A thread is suspended by an invocation of the method suspend() in class ThreadCB. When the page becomes valid, execution continues past the suspend() statement. Keep in mind that since a long time may pass between the initial pagefault and the time the faulty page becomes valid, the simulator might decide to destroy the waiting thread. In this case, the dirty and referenced bit settings must not be changed. Thus, always use the `getStatus()` method to verify that the thread does not have status `ThreadKill`.

In the second case, the method must initiate a pagefault. Unlike in the `do_lock()` method, a pagefault interrupt must be caused. It is not enough to just invoke the method `handlePagefault()` because at the time when the thread executes `refer()`, the machine is in the user mode executing a user thread. In contrast, when pagefault is caused by the `lock()` operation, the machine must already be in kernel mode, since `lock()` is called by the operating system itself.

To cause an interrupt, one must suitably set the various static fields of the class `InterruptVector`. This is done using the static methods `setPage()`, `setReferenceType()`, and `setThread()`. Then one must call the `interrupt()` method of class `CPU` and pass it the the type of the interrupt (i.e., `PageFault`). Eventually, this will invoke the method `do_handlePageFault()` in class `PageFaultHandler`. Thus, when the `interrupt()` method returns, the page will be in the main memory and the thread will be in the ready queue.

Before exiting, `do_refer()` must set the reference and the dirty bits.

In both cases, it must be kept in mind that any thread might get killed while waiting for completion of I/O. Such is the wicked nature of the simulator. If a thread is killed, neither the dirty nor the reference bits should be changed. $\mathcal{OSP}\ \mathcal{2}$ is checking these conditions vigilantly. The method `getStatus()` should be used to determine the status of a thread.

On exit, `do_refer()` must return the referenced page.

Relevant methods defined in other classes.   Here is a summary of the methods defined in other classes, which might be used in the implementation of the methods of class `MMU`:

◇ `final static public void setInterruptType(int inter)`
                                                                   `InterruptVector`
Sets the type of the interrupt in the interrupt vector. The valid values are `PageFault`, `DiskInterrupt`, and `TimerInterrupt`.

◇ `final static public int getInterruptType()`   `InterruptVector`
Extracts the interrupt type from the interrupt vector.

◇ `final static public void setThread(ThreadCB thread)`
                                                                   `InterruptVector`
Sets the thread field in the interrupt vector so that pagefault handlers can find out who has caused the interrupt.

⋄ `final static public ThreadCB getThread()`   InterruptVector
Tells which thread has caused the interrupt.

⋄ `final static public void setReferenceType(int ref)`
                                                     InterruptVector
Sets the memory reference type in the interrupt vector. The valid types
are `MemoryRead`, `MemoryWrite`, and `MemoryLock`. Applicable to pagefaults only.

⋄ `final static public int getReferenceType()`   InterruptVector
Tells what the reference type was that caused the interrupt. Applicable
to pagefaults only.

⋄ `final public void suspend(Event event)`   ThreadCB
Suspends the thread on which this method is called and puts the thread
on the waiting queue of `event`.

⋄ `final static public FrameTableEntry getFrame(int frameNumber)`
                                                              MMU
Returns the frame entry with the given frame number. This method is
defined in the superclass of `MMU`, and is inherited.

⋄ `final static public void setFrame(int index,`
`FrameTableEntry entry)`   MMU
Sets the frame with the given index to a non-null `FrameTableEntry`-
object. This method is defined in the superclass of `MMU`, and is inherited.

⋄ `final static public int getFrameTableSize()`   MMU
Returns the number of frames in the simulated machine. This method
is defined in the superclass of `MMU`, and is inherited.

⋄ `final public ThreadCB getValidatingThread()`   PageTableEntry
Returns the validating thread of the page.

⋄ `final public void setValidatingThread(ThreadCB thread)`
                                                     PageTableEntry
Sets the validating thread of the page.

Summary of Class `MMU`

The memory-management unit defines the hardware characteristics of the simulated computer. These characteristics and their access methods are described
below.

Frame table: The table whose entries describe the individual main memory
frames in $\mathcal{OSP}$ 2. The methods provided for accessing this table are:
`getFrame()`, which returns a frame object at a given index in the frame

table; `setFrame()`, which sets a frame table entry with the given index; `getFrameTableSize()`, which returns the number of entries in the frame table (i.e., the number of main-memory frames in the system). These methods can be used to traverse the frame table in a `for`-loop.

Number of bits in a virtual address: The number of bits determines the maximum addressable space in the simulated computer. For instance, 16 bits yield 2^{16} bytes of addressable space (64Kb). The method to find out this value is `getVirtualAddressBits()`.

Number of bits used to represent the offset within pages: This property directly affects the size of the pages (and frames) in the computer. For instance, 10 bits lead to 1Kb pages, while 12 bits mean that the pages are 4Kb large. The method to find out this value is `getPageAddressBits()`.

Page table base register: This register points to the page table of the running task. It is available through the methods `getPTBR()` and `setPTBR()`.

5.7 Class `PageFaultHandler`

This class contains only one method that you are required to implement as part of the project. However, you might want to define additional methods to make the implementation more modular.

◇ `public static int do_handlePageFault(ThreadCB thread, int referenceType, PageTableEntry page)`

This is the actual pagefault handler. The `thread` and the `page` arguments are the thread and the page that caused the pagefault. The `referenceType` argument can be `MemoryRead`, `MemoryWrite`, or `MemoryLock`; it represents the type of memory reference that caused the pagefault. Knowing the type of memory reference is needed to set the dirty bit correctly. If the pagefault was caused by locking (in method `do_lock()` of `PageTableEntry`), the reference type must be `MemoryLock`. Note that locking does not modify the contents of a page, so the page should *not* be marked dirty due to this type of memory reference.

The implementation of this method follows the general outline of pagefault processing described earlier. However, it is also necessary to check several exception conditions. First, the pagefault handler might be called incorrectly by the other methods in this project. So, always check if the page that is passed as a parameter is valid (already has a page frame assigned to it) and return `FAILURE` if it is. Second, it is possible that all frames are either locked or reserved and so it is not possible to find a victim page to evict and free up a frame. Return `NotEnoughMemory` if this is the case. Third, the thread that caused the pagefault can be killed by the simulator at any moment after the thread goes to sleep waiting for the swap-out or swap-in to complete. `FAILURE` should be returned in these cases.

The first two exceptional conditions must be checked at the beginning of pagefault processing, and the tests for destroyed threads must be done right after each swap-out and swap-in. In any case, before exiting, all threads that might be waiting on the page (see the explanations for `lock()` and `refer()`) must be notified using the `notifyThreads()` method of class `Event`. Finally, `dispatch()` must be called.

In case of an exception, you should always think of the appropriate ways to handle the various bits associated with pages and frames. For instance, if the thread that caused the pagefault was killed while waiting for a swap-out, we cannot be sure whether the frame has become clean or not. So, the dirty bit should not be changed in such a case.

The normal processing of a pagefault goes as follows. First, the thread must be suspended on a `SystemEvent` object created with the help of the `SystemEvent()` constructor. This event object must be saved in a variable, because when pagefault handling is finished you must resume the thread by executing `notifyThreads()` on that event.

Next, a suitable frame must be found *and reserved* to protect it from theft by other invocations of the pagefault handler (on behalf of other threads). If the frame is free, the page's frame attribute can be updated and a swap-in operation can be performed right away. If the frame contains a clean page, the frame should be freed (explained below) and then a swap-in operation should be performed. If the frame contains a dirty page, then swap-out must be performed, followed by freeing the frame, followed by a swap-in. If all is well and the thread was not killed while waiting for the two I/O operations, you update the page table (explained below) to indicate that **page** is now valid and the frame table to indicate that the newly freed frame is now occupied by **page**. Finally, the following actions must be performed:

— the frame used to satisfy the pagefault should be un-reserved

— the threads that might be waiting on **page** should be notified using `notifyThreads()`

— the thread that caused the pagefault must be resumed by executing `notifyThreads()` on the system event that you used to suspend the thread just after the entry into the pagefault handler

– `dispatch()` must be called

– SUCCESS should be returned.

Freeing frames: To free a frame, one should indicate that the frame does not hold any page (i.e., it holds the `null` page) using the `setPage()` method. The dirty and the reference bits should be set to `false`.

Updating a page table: To indicate that a page P is no longer valid, one must set its frame to `null` (using the `setFrame()` method) and the validity bit to `false` (using the `setValid()` method). To indicate that the page P has become valid and is now occupying a main memory frame F, you do the following:

– use `setFrame()` to set the frame of P to F

– use `setPage()` to set F's page to P

– set the P's validity flag correctly

– set the dirty and reference flags in F appropriately.

Performing a swap-in: This is done by issuing a read command on the swap file of the task that owns the page.

Performing a swap-out: This is done with the write command on the swap file of the task that owns the page.[3]

`read()` is a method of class `OpenFile` that is invoked on an `OpenFile`-object (which in our case is an open-file handle of a swap file) and takes three arguments: the *block number* in the file that is to be read, the *page* into which the file block is to be placed, and the *thread* that initiated the I/O. All these parameters can be obtained using the methods listed below. The only peculiarity is that a swap file contains an exact image of the task's memory, so there is a one-to-one correspondence between the pages and the blocks in the swap file. In other words, the block number should be equal to the page id.

`write()` is also a method in class `OpenFile` that is invoked on an open-file handle and takes the same arguments as `read()`.

Both `read()` and `write()` are blocking operations, i.e., they block the execution of the current thread until the I/O is finished.

Earlier we mentioned the method `getValidatingThread()`, which can be used to find out if a particular page is in the middle of a pagefault. It should

---

[3] Note: It must be the task of the page, not of the thread. Indeed, in case of a swap out, the thread and the page might belong to different tasks. Think why.

be emphasized, however, that it is the responsibility of the pagefault handler
(i.e., your implementation) to maintain the validating threads correctly. In
particular, when a pagefault occurs you must set the validating thread to be
the thread that caused the pagefault and set it to null when the pagefault is
over. All this is done with the help of the method setValidatingThread() of
the class PageTableEntry. It should also be mentioned that OSP 2 monitors
the validating thread field in every page and issues error messages when it is
incorrect. In particular, if a pagefault must occur and the validating thread
of a page stays null, it might complain that your implementation missed the
interrupt.

Relevant methods defined in other classes.   In addition to the relevant
methods listed earlier, the following methods are used in handling pagefaults:

◇ public final boolean isReserved()   FrameTableEntry
   Tests if the frame is reserved.

◇ public final boolean isDirty()   FrameTableEntry
   Tells if the frame is dirty by checking the "dirty" bit of the frame.

◇ public final void isReferenced()   FrameTableEntry
   Checks the reference bit and tells if the frame has been referenced.

◇ public final OpenFile getSwapFile()   TaskCB
   Returns the open swap file of the task. This swap file is then used in the
   read() and write() statements to perform the swap-in and swap-out
   operations. The swap file is represented by the OpenFile class, which is
   a handle that contains information about the disk blocks used by the file
   and some runtime information about the current status of the file. This
   operation blocks the current thread until the I/O operation is finished.

◇ final public void read(int blockNumber,
   PageTableEntry memoryPage,ThreadCB thread)   OpenFile
   This method is invoked on an open-file handle (which is an instance
   of class OpenFile). It reads block blockNumber from the file (specified by an open-file handle) into page memoryPage on behalf of thread.
   The open-file handle mentioned above is an object of class OpenFile.
   In our concrete case, it would be a handle of a swap file. Since here
   read() is used for swapping pages into the memory, blocks in the swap
   file must directly correspond to pages in the main memory. Therefore
   blockNumber is determined by the ID of memoryPage. This operation
   blocks the current thread until the I/O operation is finished.

◇ final public void write(int blockNumber,
   PageTableEntry memoryPage,ThreadCB thread)   OpenFile

This method is invoked on an open-file handle (which is an instance of class `OpenFile`). It writes page `memoryPage` to block `blockNumber` of the file on behalf of `thread`. As in the case of `read()`, `blockNumber` is determined by the ID of `memoryPage`.

⋄ `public void notifyThreads()`   Event
Resumes all threads that might be waiting on the event. In pagefault handling, these are the threads that might be waiting on the page that has caused a pagefault and is being swapped in.

⋄ `final public void suspend(Event event)`   ThreadCB
Suspends the thread that calls this method, placing it on the waiting queue of `event`.

⋄ `final static public void dispatch()`   ThreadCB
Dispatches a thread.

⋄ `final public ThreadCB getValidatingThread()`   PageTableEntry
Returns the validating thread of the page.

⋄ `final public void setValidatingThread(ThreadCB thread)`
                                                           PageTableEntry
Sets the validating thread of the page. Note that you have to make sure that the validating thread of a page is set correctly by the pagefault handler. In other words, you must set the page's validating thread using `setValidatingThread()` when a pagefault happens and you must set it back to null when the pagefault is over.

⋄ `final public static int handlePageFault (ThreadCB thread,`
`int referenceType, PageTableEntry page)`   PageFaultHandler
Invokes the pagefault handler. Returns `SUCCESS` if the pagefault has been handled successfully. Otherwise (for instance, it there is not enough memory) returns `FAILURE`.

⋄ `public SystemEvent(String name)`   SystemEvent
Constructor for system events. Used to create an event on which to suspend a thread at the beginning of pagefault processing. The argument, `name`, is a string that will appear in the system log and can help distinguish this event from other types of `SystemEvent`.

⋄ `static public void create(String name,`
`DaemonInterface work, int interval)`   Daemon
Used to register a daemon with the system. See Section 1.7 for details.

In addition most of the methods in class `FrameTableEntry` (such as `getPage()`, `setReserved()`, etc.) are required for the implementation of the $\mathcal{OSP}$ 2 pagefault handler.

Summary of Class `PageFaultHandler`

This class does not maintain important data structures of its own. However, it plays a central role in memory management by initiating the I/O operations that swap pages in and out of the system and by maintaining the page tables of the running processes and the frame table of the entire system.

5.8 Methods Exported by Package MEMORY

The following public methods are defined in the classes of the MEMORY package. They are useful for implementing other student modules and are also used to implement the methods that are part of the current project. To the right of each method we list the class of the objects to which the method applies.

⋄ `static public PageTable getPTBR()`   MMU

Returns the page table base register of the MMU, which is supposed to point to the page table of the currently running thread; or it is `null` if no thread is running.

⋄ `static public void setPTBR(PageTable table)`   MMU

This method changes the value of the page table base register.

⋄ `static public int getVirtualAddressBits()`   MMU

Returns the number of bits used to represent an address. This method is defined in `If1MMU` and is inherited.

⋄ `static public int getPageAddressBits()`   MMU

Returns the number of bits used to represent the page-number portion of an address. This method is defined in `If1MMU` and is inherited.

⋄ `public final boolean isValid()`   PageTableEntry

Tells if the page is valid by checking the validity bit.

⋄ `public final void setValid(boolean flag)`   PageTableEntry

Sets the validity bit of the page to `flag`.

Notice that there is a difference between setting the valid flag and setting the frame of a page (using `setFrame()`). The frame is set just before the swap-in operation so that the I/O subsystem will know which frame to load the page into. The method `setValid()` is used only after this operation is complete.

⋄ `public final FrameTableEntry getFrame()`   PageTableEntry

Returns the frame of the page (or `null`).

⋄ `public final void setFrame(FrameTableEntry frame)`

PageTableEntry

Sets the frame of the page to `frame`. If the page is being evicted, then `frame` is `null`.

`setFrame()` must be called before swapping in a page and after the page becomes invalid. In the former case, you need to set the frame of the page to tell the I/O subsystem where to put the page. The validity bit of the page should be set only after the page is loaded.

◇ `public final int getID()`   PageTableEntry
  Returns the ID of the page.

◇ `public final TaskCB getTask()`   PageTableEntry
  Returns the task that owns the page.

◇ `final public ThreadCB getValidatingThread()`   PageTableEntry
  Returns the validating thread of the page.

◇ `final public void setValidatingThread(ThreadCB thread)`
                                                PageTableEntry

  Sets the validating thread of the page.

◇ `public final void isReferenced()`   FrameTableEntry
  Checks the reference bit and tells if the frame has been referenced.

◇ `public final void setReferenced(boolean flag)`   FrameTableEntry
  Sets the reference bit to the value of `flag`.

◇ `public final boolean isDirty()`   FrameTableEntry
  Tells if the frame is dirty by checking the "dirty" bit of the frame.

◇ `public final void setReserved(TaskCB t)`   FrameTableEntry
  Sets the frame as reserved by task t.

◇ `public final TaskCB getReserved()`   FrameTableEntry
  Returns the task that has reserved this frame or `null`.

◇ `public final void setUnreserved(TaskCB t)`   FrameTableEntry
  Un-reserves the frame previously reserved by task t; error, if the frame is not reserved by t.

◇ `public final void setDirty(boolean flag)`   FrameTableEntry
  Sets the dirty bit to `flag`.

◇ `public PageTableEntry pages[]`   PageTable
  This is the array that represents the page table. It must be initialized by the page table constructor described in Section 5.5.

◇ `public final TaskCB getTask()`   PageTable
  Returns the owner task of the page table.

DEVICES: *Scheduling of Disk Requests*

6.1 Chapter Objective

The objective of project DEVICES is to teach students about device I/O and, relatedly, certain aspects of device drivers. One main focus will be the scheduling of disk I/O requests. To meet these objectives, students will be asked to implement the three public classes of the DEVICES package: `Device`, `IORB`, and `DiskInterruptHandler`. The class `Device` deals with the scheduling of I/O requests, `IORB` implements the I/O Request Block data structure, and `DiskInterruptHandler` constitutes the interrupt handler for I/O devices.

6.2 Overview of I/O Handling

I/O supervisor and I/O Request Block.　　When the user thread issues a `read()` or `write()` system call, the OS assembles an **input/output request block** (or **IORB**) and passes the request to the basic I/O supervisor: the portion of the operating system responsible for managing the various I/O devices of the system. The IORB includes information about the thread that issued the call; the buffer page in main memory that contains the data to be written out or into which the data is to be copied from the secondary storage; the disk block to which the buffer data is to be written out or which contains the data to be read in; and the I/O device that is the target of the requested

I/O operation.

The I/O supervisor examines the IORB and places it on the **device queue** of the targeted device. A device queue is nothing more than a queue of waiting-to-be-serviced IORBs, one such queue per I/O device in the system.

Disk interrupt handler.   When the device finishes servicing an I/O request, a device interrupt occurs, which is the way by which external devices notify the CPU about completion of an I/O operation. The eventual result of an I/O interrupt is that the appropriate device interrupt handler is called. In $OSP\,2$ the only external devices are disks, so the only device interrupt handler is the disk interrupt handler.

A disk interrupt handler performs a variety of functions, which we will describe in detail in Section 6.5. One of these is to invoke the I/O scheduler, which chooses the IORB to be serviced next, assuming the device queue is non-empty; i.e. contains at least one IORB. Once an IORB has been selected, it is dequeued from the device queue and the device is instructed to process the request. If the device queue is empty, the device simply idles.

Disk-scheduling algorithms.   A variety of disk-scheduling policies have been proposed for use by the I/O scheduler. Many of these policies are concerned with performance and QoS (Quality of Service) issues related to the physical characteristics of a disk device. Such a device is typically configured as a number of platters, each of which has an upper and lower surface on which data can be magnetically encoded. A surface consists of a number of concentric tracks each of which is divided into storage regions known as sectors. For most disk drives, a fixed sector size of 512 bytes is used. The block size of a disk is the number of bytes transferred in a single I/O operation, and is usually a multiple of the sector size. The preceding discussion therefore tells us that a disk address consists of a surface number, track number, and sector number.

Each surface has its own disk arm, at the end of which is a read/write head that must be positioned over the appropriate track for an I/O operation to occur. The arms are attached to the disk-drive boom, which moves the arms in unison back and forth over the tracks of the various surfaces. This gives rise to the concept of the disk cylinder: the collection of tracks carved out of 3-space by virtue of having all read/write heads positioned over the same-numbered track on all surfaces.

Disk I/O can be slow compared with say the time it takes the CPU to access main memory due to the electromechanical aspects of disk operation. In particular, having to position the disk arm over the correct track before an I/O can take place is the biggest culprit. The time taken by this movement is called the **seek time** and many proposed disk-scheduling strategies seek to minimize this delay. **Rotational delay**, the time spent waiting for the proper sector to circle under the read/write head, is another overhead of disk I/O but of much less concern to us since it is about an order of magnitude smaller than the seek time.

Some of the most well-known disk-scheduling algorithms are:

Shortest Seek Time First (SSTF) Services the IORB that requires the least movement of the disk arm from its current position.

SCAN The arm is moved in one direction only, satisfying all outstanding requests en route until it reaches the last track in that direction. The service direction is then reversed and the scan proceeds in the opposite direction.

LOOK A variant of SCAN where the service direction is reversed when there are no more requests in the current service direction (rather than proceeding to the last track).

C-SCAN A variant of SCAN which restricts scanning to one direction only. When the last track has been visited in that direction, the arm is returned to the opposite end of the disk and the scan begins again.

C-LOOK The variant of LOOK in which scanning is restricted to one direction, just as in C-SCAN.

Priority Unlike the above algorithms, this approach is not intended to optimize disk utilization but rather to meet other system objectives. For example, it may give priority to IORBs coming from interactive processes rather than those from computationally intensive batch jobs, with the goal of providing good interactive response time.

It is important to note that *OSP 2* disks do not support the command that moves the read/write head to a specified cylinder without starting an I/O. The head moves only when the `startIO()` command is issued. It is therefore not possible to implement strategies such as SCAN and LOOK which require the head to be moved to the first and last cylinders even when there are no outstanding I/O requests to these cylinders.

Synchronous versus asynchronous I/O. To conclude our discussion of disk-scheduling strategies, let us consider a relatively new disk-scheduling algorithm that has exhibited superior performance on web-server and file-system benchmarks. *Anticipatory scheduling* is useful in the context of synchronous I/O, where a thread that has issued an I/O operation is blocked until the I/O completes. In contrast, with asynchronous I/O, a thread initiates an I/O operation and then can continue processing while the I/O request is fulfilled.

I/O in $\mathcal{OSP}$ 2 is of the synchronous variety, although it is possible to simulate asynchronous I/O in $\mathcal{OSP}$ 2; see Section 7.7.

Seek-optimizing algorithms can get confused by synchronous I/O since in this case threads issue one I/O request at a time (after the previous request has finished). Thus the scheduler may incorrectly assume that the thread issuing the last I/O request has momentarily no further I/O requests and therefore selects a request from another thread. This is a bad decision on the part of the scheduler if the current thread is requesting data sequentially positioned on the disk which is often the case in practice. Anticipatory scheduling seeks to mitigate this problem by issuing a short, controlled delay period before selecting the next IORB to be serviced. This allows the thread that issued the last request to issue additional requests before the next scheduling decision is made.

In the rest of this section we provide a detailed description of the classes that comprise the package DEVICES. Figure 6.1 places these classes in the overall context of $\mathcal{OSP}$ 2.

6.3 Class IORB

Before discussing the workings of the I/O supervisor, we need to look more closely at the structure of an IORB. The class for this data structure is defined as follows:

◇ public class IORB extends IflIORB

and its only mandatory method has a six-argument constructor:

◇ public IORB(ThreadCB thread, PageTableEntry page, int blockNumber, int deviceID, int ioType, OpenFile openFile)
  As usual for $\mathcal{OSP}$ 2 class constructors, the first thing this class does is call super() with the same set of arguments. The rest depends on your implementation. For instance, if you define additional fields in this class, you can initialize them in the constructor.

As follows from the argument list, an IORB keeps information about the thread which issued the request, the buffer page involved, the device and the device's block that contains the data to be read in or on which the page is to be written out, the type of I/O operation (which can be either MemoryRead or MemoryWrite, two predefined constants in $\mathcal{OSP}$ 2), and the open-file handle. The last of these arguments will be defined in more detail in Chapter 7. For now it suffices to know that an open-file handle contains runtime information, such as the file size and the list of blocks allocated to the file, which the OS

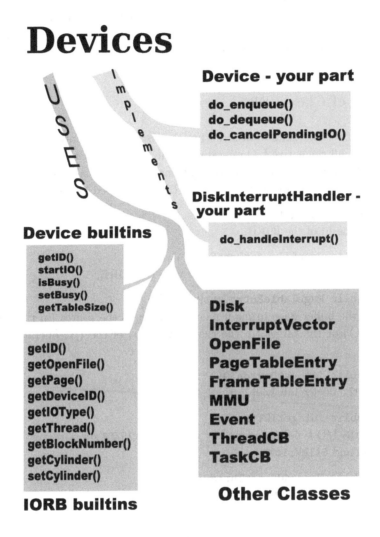

Figure 6.1 An overview of the package DEVICES.

needs in order to process I/O operations on that file. This handle comes from one of the parameters of the read() or write() system call that created the IORB in question.

It is important to keep in mind that IORB is also a subclass of Event so threads can wait on it and be notified. See Section 1.6 to refresh your memory about *OSP 2* events.

Relevant methods defined in other classes.   Typically, implementation of this class does not use methods provided by other $\mathcal{OSP}$ 2 classes, since the only mandatory method in this class is the constructor and the components of an IORB can be queried via the built-ins provided by $\mathcal{OSP}$ 2 itself (see below).

Summary of Class IORB

This class defines the IORB data structure that is used to maintain the information about all the active I/O operations. The following API can be used to query an IORB. All these methods are built-ins that apply to an IORB object and they return the components of that IORB as described below.

⋄ final public int getID()
   Provides the Id of the IORB.

⋄ final public OpenFile getOpenFile()
   Returns the open-file handle associated with the IORB.

⋄ final public PageTableEntry getPage()
   Returns the buffer page in main memory, which is the source (in the case of write()) or the target (in the case of read()) of the I/O operation in question.

⋄ final public int getDeviceID()
   Returns the device involved in the I/O operation.

⋄ final public int getIOType()
   Returns the I/O type represented by the IORB. $\mathcal{OSP}$ 2 supports two types: FileRead and FileWrite.

⋄ final public ThreadCB getThread()
   Returns the thread that requested the I/O.

⋄ final public int getBlockNumber()
   Returns the block number of the device, which is the source (in the case of read()) or the target (in the case of write()) of the I/O.

⋄ public final void setCylinder(int cylinder)
   Sets the target disk cylinder for this IORB to cylinder. This is done in do_enqueueIORB() in Device. This method is used by $\mathcal{OSP}$ 2 to make sure that both it and the student module calculate the cylinders associated with IORBs the same way.

⋄ public final int getCylinder()
   Returns the target cylinder associated with this IORB. Since the IORB

cylinder is set in `do_enqueueIORB()`, `getCylinder()` can be used only in `do_dequeueIORB()`.

6.4 Class `Device`

This class implements the I/O scheduler and performs other functions, such as starting I/O operations on devices. The following methods are part of the project and must be implemented by the student.

⋄ `public static void init()`
This method is called at the very beginning of the simulation and can be used to initialize static variables that might exist in the student program.

⋄ `public Device(int id, int numberOfBlocks)`
This is the class constructor. It must call `super(id,numberOfBlocks)` and then initialize the device object. One thing that requires initialization is the variable `iorbQueue` described later in this section.

⋄ `public int do_enqueueIORB(IORB iorb)`
This method is executed on a device object and puts `iorb` on the waiting queue of that device. When programming this method, however, you must first perform several tasks before the enqueueing. First, you must lock the page associated with the `iorb` using the `lock()` method of class `PageTable-Entry`. This is done in order to ensure that the page will not be swapped out from now till the end of the I/O operation. (If this page is not currently in main memory, `lock()` will cause a pagefault, which will eventually bring the page into main memory.)

Second, you must increment the IORB count of the open-file handle associated with `iorb`. This is accomplished using method `incrementIORBCount()` of class `OpenFile`. Because different threads can issue I/O operations concurrently on the same file, $\mathcal{OSP}\,2$ needs to maintain a count of IORBs that are active for each open-file handle. Knowing the count allows it to ensure that files cannot be closed before all the outstanding I/O operations have finished. (Closing a file deallocates its file handle, which can cause havoc since outstanding IORBs for this file reference the handle.)

Third, you must set the `iorb`'s cylinder, using method `setCylinder()`, to the cylinder that contains the disk block mentioned in the IORB.

You are now ready to enqueue the IORB but not before you check that the thread that requested the I/O is still alive (using the `getStatus()` method of class `ThreadCB`), i.e., its status is not `ThreadKill`. If the thread has died, method `do_enqueueIORB()` should return `FAILURE`.

If the thread is alive and the device is idle (you can check for idleness by executing the method `isBusy()` on the device), you can start the I/O operation immediately using the method `startIO()` on the device object and passing it the `iorb` as a parameter. The method `do_enqueueIORB()` should then return `SUCCESS` and exit.

If the device is busy, then put the `iorb` on the device queue and exit by returning `SUCCESS`. The device queue is represented by the variable `iorbQueue` that can take any object that implements the type `GenericQueueInterface` (Section 1.5), as described later in this section.

Disk I/O scheduling is typically implemented as part of this method as the different scheduling strategies work best with differently structured device queues. For instance, for the C-SCAN strategy, the IORBs in the queue might need to be ordered according to the cylinder numbers that contain the requested disk blocks. In this case, sorting would be best done when IORBs are enqueued.

◇ `public IORB do_dequeueIORB()`
This method selects an IORB from the device queue according to some scheduling strategy, deletes it from the queue, and returns the selected IORB. If the queue is empty, `null` is returned.

The I/O scheduling strategy (or parts of it) can also be implemented in this method, because ultimately it is this method that chooses the requests to be serviced. *OSP 2* does not mandate any particular way of implementing scheduling.

Note that you should *not* unlock the page used by the dequeued IORB. This is because the device has not finished servicing the IORB, so the page must stay locked. It will eventually be unlocked when the device finishes servicing the request and the device interrupt occurs.

◇ `public void do_cancelPendingIO(ThreadCB thread)`
The purpose of this method is to iterate over the device queue removing all IORBs initiated by `thread`. The need to do this arises when a thread is killed. This prevents the device from servicing requests that nobody wants any more.

For each IORB associated with `thread` found in the queue, you must unlock the buffer page used by that IORB. Indeed, when the IORB was enqueued, the corresponding page was locked. Normally it would be unlocked in the device interrupt handler after the request is serviced. However, since you are removing the IORB from the device queue, this request will never be serviced, so you must unlock the page here.

In addition, you must decrement the IORB count of the open-file handle associated with the IORB. Again, normally this is done in the device interrupt handler, but because the IORB in question will never be serviced, you must decrement the count here.

Finally, you should *try* to close the open-file handle associated with the IORB. To understand why, let us consider what happens when a thread is trying to issue a `close()` system call on a file handle. If the handle does not have associated IORBs, the file is closed and the handle is deleted. However, if there are outstanding IORBs for the handle, the system sets the `closePending` flag for that handle, but does not close the file in order to allow the outstanding I/O requests to execute.[1] When all such I/O requests have finished, the file is closed. One of the places where the `closePending` flag should be checked is in the `do_cancelPendingIO()` method. Indeed, if the file was not closed due to outstanding I/O requests and now you are canceling all the outstanding IORBs belonging to `thread`, it is possible that the file handle has no remaining IORBs, so it can be closed. In other words, when removing an IORB associated with `thread` you must check the `closePending` flag of the open-file handle of the IORB. If it is set to *true* and the count of IORBs for this handle has become 0, the file handle must be closed with the `close()` method of `OpenFile`. To check the current count of pending IORBs for a file handle use the method `getIORBCount()` of class `OpenFile`.

How to compute a cylinder from a block.   Many scheduling strategies require you to compute a cylinder from a given block number. To do this, you first need to compute the number of blocks in a track.

A track consists of a number of blocks, which in turn consists of a number of sectors. To find the block size, you can use the functions `getVirtualAddress-Bits()` and `getPageAddressBits()`, since the size of a disk block equals the size of a main-memory page. The block size together with the sector size (`getBytesPerSector()`) gives the number of sectors in a block.

The number of blocks per track can be used to compute the track that holds the given block. To compute the cylinder number corresponding to the block you need to know the number of tracks per cylinder. In $\mathcal{OSP}$ *2* we assume

---

[1] You may have faced this issue while implementing the `kill()` method of `TaskCB`, which destroys a task. One job that this method is tasked with is closing all open files owned by the task. You may have experienced the unexpected effect of the `close()` system call where some open-file handles stayed around after being closed. The reason for this was the presence of outstanding IORBs.

that each disk platter is one sided, so the number of tracks in a cylinder equals the number of platters in the disk. The latter is obtained using the method getPlatters().

Relevant methods defined in other classes.   The following methods defined in other modules are used by the methods in class Device.

◇ public final int lock(IORB iorb)   PageTableEntry
When executed on a page object, this methods locks that page in main memory, so it cannot be swapped out.

◇ public final void unlock()   PageTableEntry
Unlocks the page that was previously locked by the lock() method.

◇ final public void incrementIORBCount()   OpenFile
Increments the count of IORBs active for the given file handle.

◇ final public void decrementIORBCount()   OpenFile
Decrements the IORB count for the given file handle.

◇ final public int getIORBCount()   OpenFile
Returns the current IORB count for the open-file handle.

◇ final public void close()   OpenFile
Closes the open-file handle.

◇ final public int getStatus()   ThreadCB
Returns the status of a thread. In this case you need to know when a thread is killed. The status of a killed thread is ThreadKill.

◇ static final public int getVirtualAddressBits()   MMU
Returns the number of bits used to specify a virtual address.

◇ static final public int getPageAddressBits()   MMU
Returns the number of bits used to specify a page address. From this and the number of bits in a virtual address one can compute the size of a memory page (and of a disk block).

◇ public final void setCylinder(int cylinder)   IORB
Sets the cylinder of the IORB to cylinder.

◇ public final int getCylinder()   IORB
Returns the cylinder previously set by setCylinder(). Since the IORB cylinder is set in do_enqueueIORB(), getCylinder() can be used only in do_dequeueIORB().

In addition, the following methods, implemented in class Disk, are available. These methods can be useful in order to implement certain I/O scheduling strategies. Note that `Disk` is a subclass of `Device`. Since the devices we are dealing with in this project are disks, all these methods are applicable to the `Device` objects that occur in this project.

◇ `final public int getHeadPosition()`
Returns the head position (the cylinder number where the read/write head is parked). Cylinders are counted from 0.

◇ `final public int getPlatters()`
Returns the number of platters in the disk.

◇ `final public int getTracksPerPlatter()`
Tells how many tracks a platter has (or, equivalently, the number of cylinders on the disk).

◇ `final public int getSectorsPerTrack()`
Tells the number of sectors per track.

◇ `final public int getBytesPerSector()`
Returns the number of bytes per sector.

◇ `final public int getRevsPerTick()`
Returns the number of revolutions of the disk per tick.

◇ `final public int getSeekTimePerCylinder()`
Tells how long it takes to seek to the next cylinder.

Summary of Class `Device`

The following API provided by class `Device` (implemented in its superclasses) can be used to obtain information about $\mathcal{OSP}$ 2 devices. All the methods and variables listed apply to `Device` objects.

◇ `protected GenericQueueInterface iorbQueue`
This variable holds the device queue. It is manipulated by the methods `do_enqueueIORB()` and `do_dequeueIORB()`. The implementation of the device queue is *up to the student* module. The only requirement is that the class of the queue object must implement the interface `GenericQueue-Interface`. This interface mandates the methods `length()`, `isEmpty()`, and `contains()`, as described at the end of Section 1.5. Note that the interface defines only the methods $\mathcal{OSP}$ 2 itself uses internally. For your purposes, your queue class would need additional methods, such as insertion and deletion of members of the queue. Note that since these methods are not defined in `GenericQueueInterface` you would need to use the *cast* operator to invoke them on `iorbQueue`.

⋄ `final public boolean isBusy()`
Tests if the device is busy.

⋄ `final public void setBusy(boolean flag)`
Sets the device busy or idle depending on the value of `flag`.

⋄ `final static public Device get(int deviceID)`
Returns the device object with the given device Id.

⋄ `final public int getID()`
Returns the Id of the device.

⋄ `final public void startIO(IORB iorb)`
Starts the device and instructs it to perform the I/O operation specified in `iorb`. As part of this operation the device becomes busy, so you do not need to set it to busy explicitly.

⋄ `final public String ospDeviceQueue()`
This method returns a string that contains the OSP version of the waiting queue to the device. You can print it out and use it for debugging.

⋄ `final public int getTableSize()`
Returns the size of the device table.

6.5 Class `DiskInterruptHandler`

This class is declared as follows:

```
public class DiskInterruptHandler extends IflDiskInterruptHandler
```

It has only one method, `do_handleInterrupt()`, which implements the device interrupt handler. The method has the following signature:

```
public void do_handleInterrupt()
```

The following actions need to be performed as part of the handler:

1. Obtain information about the interrupt from the interrupt vector, class `InterruptVector`, described in Section 1.4. The main piece of information is the IORB that caused the interrupt. It is obtained using the method `getEvent()` of class `InterruptVector` (since the IORB is the event that "caused" the interrupt). The other necessary pieces of information, the thread, page, open-file handle, etc., are obtained using the API described in Section 6.3.

2. The IORB count of the open-file handle associated with the IORB must be decremented using `decrementIORBCount()` as described earlier.

3. If the open file has the `closePending` flag set and the IORB count is 0, the file might need to be closed. The IORB count of a file handle can be obtained via the method `getIORBCount()`. See the relevant part of the description of the method `do_cancelPendingIO()`.

4. The page associated with the IORB must be unlocked, because the I/O operation (due to which the page was locked) is over.

5. If the I/O operation is *not* a page swap-in or swap-out, then, unless the thread that created the IORB is dead, you need to set the frame associated with the IORB's page as referenced using the method `setReferenced()` of `FrameTableEntry`. In addition if it was a read operation (I/O type `FileRead`) then the frame must be set dirty (using the method `setDirty()` of `FrameTableEntry`). Of course, this can only be done if the task associated with the thread is still alive, as otherwise the memory of the task will be deallocated anyway. The thread's task is obtained using the method `getTask()` and its status is checked using the method `getStatus()`. A live task has status `TaskLive`; otherwise, the status is `TaskTerm`.

   To find out whether an I/O is a swap-in or swap-out from/to the swap device, one should compare the device Id of the IORB (`getDeviceID()`) with `SwapDeviceID`, a constant defined in $\mathcal{OSP}\ 2$.

6. If the I/O was directed to the swap device and the task that owns the thread and the IORB is alive, you should mark the frame as clean (`setDirty(false)`).

7. If the task that owns the IORB is dead (status `TaskTerm`) and the frame associated with the IORB was reserved by that task (verified using `getReserved()`), you must unreserve the frame using `setUnreserved()`.

8. The threads that are waiting on the IORB must be woken up by a call to `notifyThreads()`.

9. The device must be set to idle using the method `setBusy()` with the appropriate flag.

10. The device must be told to service a new I/O request. This IORB is picked up using the method `dequeueIORB()`. If it returns a non-null object, the device should be restarted with that IORB using the method `startIO()`.

11. Finally, a new thread must be dispatched using method `dispatch()` of `ThreadCB`.

Relevant methods defined in other classes. The following methods defined in other modules can be used to implement the disk interrupt handler.

◇ `final static public Event getEvent()`   `InterruptVector`
  Extracts the event that caused the interrupt (e.g., a page, an IORB).

◇ `final static public ThreadCB getThread()`   `InterruptVector`
  Returns the thread that caused the interrupt.

◇ `final public void decrementIORBCount()`   `OpenFile`
  Decrements the count of active IORBs associated with the open-file handle.

◇ `final public int getIORBCount()`   `OpenFile`
  Returns the current IORB count for the open-file handle.

◇ `public final void setReferenced(boolean flag)`   `FrameTableEntry`
  Marks frame as referenced.

◇ `public final void setDirty(boolean flag)`   `FrameTableEntry`
  Marks frame as dirty.

◇ `public final TaskCB getReserved()`   `FrameTableEntry`
  Marks frame as reserved.

◇ `public final void setUnreserved(TaskCB t)`   `FrameTableEntry`
  Unreserves frame.

◇ `final public int getDeviceID()`   `IORB`
  Returns the device associated with the IORB.

◇ `final public ThreadCB getThread()`   `IORB`
  Returns the thread that issued the I/O request.

◇ `final public PageTableEntry getPage()`   `IORB`
  Returns the buffer page in main memory that is the source or the target of the I/O.

◇ `public void notifyThreads()`   `Event`
  Wakes up threads that are waiting on the event.

◇ `final public void setBusy(boolean flag)`   `Device`
  If `flag` is *true*, marks the device as busy. Otherwise, marks it as idle.

◇ `final public IORB dequeueIORB()`   `Device`
  Takes an IORB off the device queue and Returns that IORB object.

◇ `final static public void startIO(IORB iorb)`   `Device`
  Tells the device to start working on iorb.

◇ `final static public void dispatch()`   `ThreadCB`
  Dispatches a thread to run.

⋄ `final public TaskCB getTask()`   ThreadCB
  Returns the task that owns the thread.

⋄ `final public int getStatus()`   ThreadCB
  Tells the status of the thread. See `GlobalVariables`, Section 1.5, for the
  list of legal status codes for a thread.

⋄ `final public int getStatus()`   TaskCB
  Tells the status of the task. See `GlobalVariables`, Section 1.5, for the list
  of legal status codes for a task.

Summary of Class `DiskInterruptHandler`

This class typically does not maintain data structures of its own. However,
since it is intended to process device interrupts, it indirectly manipulates other
data structures, such as `IORB`'s, threads, and page tables, through the methods
provided by these classes.

6.6 Methods Exported by Package DEVICES

The package DEVICES exports the following methods that are used by other
classes in $\mathcal{OSP}$ 2. To the right of each method we indicate the class where the
method is defined.

⋄ `final public ThreadCB getThread()`   IORB
  Returns the thread that requested the I/O.

⋄ `final public int getTableSize()`   IORB
  Returns the size of the device table.

⋄ `final static public Device get(int deviceID)`   IORB
  Returns the device object with the given device Id.

7

FILESYS: *The File System*

7.1 Chapter Objective

The objective of the FILESYS project is to teach students about file-system design and organization and about the management of logical, file-based I/O in a modern operating system. To this end, students will be asked to implement the five public classes of the FILESYS package: `MountTable`, which maps files to physical devices; `INode`, which keeps track of space allocation to files; `DirectoryEntry`, which defines the directory structures; `OpenFile`, which provides methods for manipulating open files via open-file handles (including the `read()` and `write()` operations); and `FileSys`, which provides a set of operations, such as `create()` and `delete()`, on non-open files.

7.2 File System Design Objectives

We briefly consider some of the main design issues in modern file systems, particularly those pertinent to the FILESYS project, and then discuss how these are addressed in *OSP 2*.

Naming. In a modern file system, users are able to refer to a file by a symbolic file name. Typically such a name is in the form of a **pathname**, a sequence of directory names ending in a target file, which can also be a directory. For example, consider the pathname /home/fac/sas/osp/filesystem.tex. This pathname starts at the root of the hierarchical file system directory structure (see discussion of directories below) indicated by the / character. The **directory separator character** / is also used to delimit names in the sequence. The target file in this case is filesystem.tex. *OSP 2* supports a hierarchical directory structure and pathnames for symbolic file naming. Pathnames can also commence from the working directory such as in osp/filesystem.tex, assuming the working directory is /home/fac/sas. The working directory can be manipulated interactively within the command shell.

The process of following the sequence of directory entries along a pathname to reach the target file is known as **pathname dereferencing**. Pathname dereferencing becomes more complicated by the presence of mountable file systems, discussed below.

Directory structures.   Early MS-DOS file systems supported *flat* file directory structures where all files resided at the same, single level. Today's directory structures are multi-level and hierarchical where directories may contain subdirectories and so on. Such hierarchies start at the *root* directory /. This does not necessarily impose a tree structure on directories as files can be *linked* to from any directory, as discussed below.

Links.   Modern file systems, Unix-style ones in particular, provide a link() system call that allows one to create a new link (directory entry) for an existing file and increment its **link count** by one. The pathname of the existing file is given as the argument to link(). If successful, link() returns the pathname of the new directory entry.

Such a directory entry is a **hard link** to the existing file, and requires that both files reside on the same file system (see discussion of mountable file systems below). Both the old and the new link share equal access and rights to the underlying object. A hard link can thus be viewed as a pointer to a file and is indistinguishable from the original directory entry. Any changes to a file are effective independent of the name used to reference the file. A hard link may not refer to directories.

A **symbolic link** is an indirect pointer to a file; its directory entry contains the name of the file to which it is linked. Symbolic links may span file systems and may refer to directories.

Mountable file systems.   Another feature of modern file systems is the mount() system call, which requests that a removable file system be **mounted** on a specified directory. Subsequent references to this directory will access the root directory (by default) of the mounted file system. The file system keeps track of mounted file systems and the directories on which they are mounted via a **mount table**. For example, suppose the root directory of a disk volume is mounted on /home/fac/sas. Then the pathname /home/fac/sas/osp/filesystem.tex ultimately references the target file named filesystem.tex on that mounted volume. Pathname dereferencing in the presence of mount tables is discussed more extensively in Section 7.4.

File storage allocation methods.   How does the file system keep track of the disk blocks allocated to a particular file? Possibilities include *contiguous allocation*, where a single contiguous set of blocks is allocated to the file at the time of file creation; *chained allocation*, where each block allocated to the file contains a pointer to the next block in the chain; and *indexed allocation*, which associates a (multi-level) index structure with the file indicating the blocks that have been allocated to the file. Indexed allocation addresses many of the problems of contiguous and chained allocation, and is used in modern operating systems such as Unix, Windows, and $\mathcal{OSP}$ 2.

Free space management.   How does the file system keep track of the free space on a disk, that is those disk blocks that can be allocated to a file whenever the need arises? Possibilities include *bit tables* which use a bit vector containing one bit for each block on the disk. An entry of 0 corresponds to a free block and an entry of 1 corresponds to a block in use. In the *chaining* method, each free portion of disk space contains a length field and a pointer to the next free portion in the chain. The *indexing* approach treats free space as a file and uses an index table as described under file allocation. The *free block list* method numbers each block sequentially and a list of all free blocks is maintained in a reserved portion of the disk.

7.3 Overview of the $\mathcal{OSP}$ 2 File System

The $\mathcal{OSP}$ 2 file system is a node-labeled tree, with support for hard links. The nodes of the tree represent files. The root node of the tree is labeled with the 1-character constant string, FileSys.DirSeparator, which can be "/" or "\". In the ensuing discussion, we shall use "/", but this should not be assumed in the student programs. The rest of the labels are strings of arbitrary characters except FileSys.DirSeparator. The labels are called **names** of files. A **full name** or the **pathname** of a file (or directory) associated with the current node is obtained by concatenating all the labels on the path from the root to that node while separating the different names with `FileSys.DirSeparator`.

A file can be a **plain file** or a **directory**. A directory is a special file that contains information about other files. These other files are **members** of the directory; they correspond to the nodes that are children of the directory node in the tree. Thus, internal nodes of the file tree can only be directories. The leaves of the tree can be either plain files or directories. A directory that appears as a leaf is said to be **empty**.

Note that directory names that differ only in `DirSeparator` at the end are considered the same; i.e., if `DirSeparator` is "/" and `/foo` is a directory then `/foo/` is considered to be the same directory. Also, multiple occurrences of the separator character can be replaced by just one occurrence. For instance, `/foo/bar` and `///foo//bar` refer to the same file.

A file (or a directory) can be created and deleted. To work with a file, a thread must first **open** it and obtain an **open-file handle**. This handle contains run-time information about the file. The read and write operations are performed on the *open-file handle* rather than on the name of a file. When a thread is done working with a file, it can **close** the file handle and thus destroy it. An open-file handle is a locus of run-time information about the file. In a typical operating system it includes (among other things) the inode of the file, the task, and the current position in the file. $\mathcal{OSP}\ 2$ does not keep the current position, but it does maintain the rest of this information.

A pathname identifies a unique file, but a file can have any number of names. In fact, a file is uniquely represented by its **inode** (index node), which contains information about the blocks allocated to the file. Pathnames are associated with inodes through **directory entries**, but a file's inode itself contains no information about the names associated with the file. To associate another name with a file, a thread can create a **hard link** to the file, which creates another association between a pathname and the file's inode.

Deleting a file does not necessarily destroy the file's inode. Instead, it destroys the directory entry that associates the inode with a particular pathname that was used as a parameter to the `delete()` operation. Each inode has an associated **hard-link count**: the number of hard links to the inode, which is also the number of distinct names associated with the file. When a delete operation is executed on a pathname associated with a particular inode, the hard-link count is decremented by one. The inode is deleted only when *both* the hard-link count and the open count (described below) become zero.

A file's inode not only keeps track of the number of hard links to the file, but also of the file's **open count**, the number of times the file has been opened. The same inode can be open multiple times because the `open()` operation can be executed on different names associated with the file (and, in fact, even on the same pathname). When this happens, a new open-file handle is allocated, and the same file can be accessed through different handles. Threads of the same task share the open-file handles, so typically they do not need to open the same file multiple times. However, different tasks might want to access the same file concurrently in which case they need separate file handles. When a file is opened through one of its pathnames, its open count is incremented by one. Closing a file (with the `close()` operation) decrements the open count by one.

We will now discuss each of the classes that belong to the package FILESYS. Figures 7.1 and 7.2 place them in the larger context of the $\mathcal{OSP}$ 2 system.

7.4 Class MountTable

Mount tables associate files with devices. For example, in Windows, a file named `C:\foo\bar` is said to be residing on device C and a file named `D:\abc\cde` is on device D. A mount table will then associate the letters C and D with particular physical devices.[1]

In Unix systems the association between devices and files is more flexible, but also more complex. First, Unix does not use letters to represent devices. Instead, devices are associated with directories. A mount table then is a relation that consists of a list of pairs of the form ⟨`pathname`, `deviceID`⟩. The `pathname` part of such a pair is called a **mountpoint**.

$\mathcal{OSP}$ 2 uses Unix-like mount tables. An example mount table is given in Figure 7.3. In that figure, we see four directories associated with four physical devices. The first question is: How does the system decide on which device any given file should reside? For example, consider the file `/foo/bar/abc/cde`. Since this file is a descendant of the root directory, `/`, and this directory is a mountpoint residing on device 0, one might think that this is where the file should live. However, this file is also in a subdirectory of mountpoint `/foo`, which lives on device 0. Looking more closely, we see that our file is also a descendant of mountpoint `/foo/bar`, which is on device 3. Which device is the correct one?

The actual mapping of files to devices works as follows. Given a full file name f, the system finds the longest name of a mountpoint d that matches f, where "matches" means that d is a prefix of f and f is a descendant of

---

[1] Typically a physical device is further subdivided into **partitions** and the drive letters (as well as directories in Unix—see below) are associated with partitions. In other words, partitions represent an intermediate layer between files and the actual devices they reside on. This intermediate layer does not exist in $\mathcal{OSP}$ 2, and we will ignore it here.

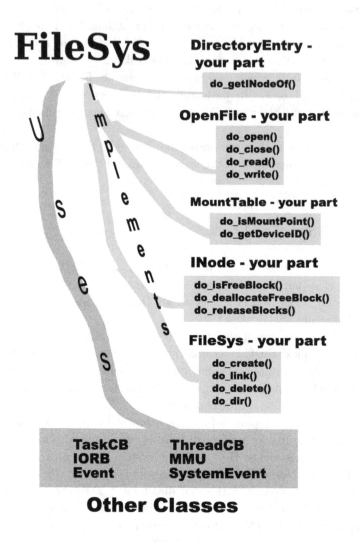

Figure 7.1 An overview of the package FILESYS, I.

d in the file-tree hierarchy. For example, the longest mountpoint in the table of Figure 7.3 that matches /foo/bar/abc/cde is /foo/bar and thus the file /foo/bar/abc/cde resides on device 3. Note that if the mount table had a pair ⟨/foo/bar/ab, 4⟩ then the mountpoint /foo/bar/ab would *not* match /foo/bar/abc/cde because the latter file does *not* reside in a subdirectory of

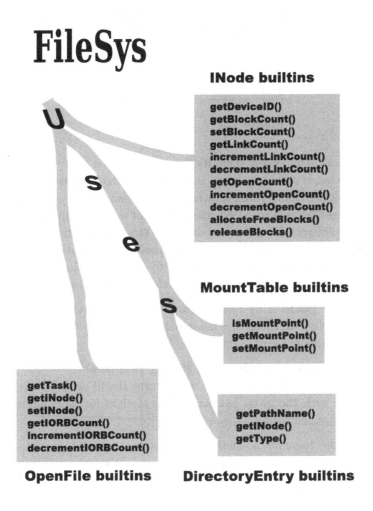

Figure 7.2 An overview of the package FILESYS, II.

/foo/bar/ab (but rather in /foo/bar/abc).[2]

The MountTable class in $\mathcal{OSP}$ 2 is intended to provide the correct mapping

---

[2] Another way to describe the matching criterion is to *standardize* all file names. A **standardized file name** is a full file name such that multiple occurrences of DirSeparator are replaced with one occurrence and if the file is a directory then DirSeparator is added at the end of the name. Given a file name f, the matching mountpoint is the one whose standardized name is the longest prefix of f.

Directory name	Device ID
/foo	0
/swap	2
/foo/bar	3
/	1

Figure 7.3 A mount table.

of files to devices. The mount table itself is encapsulated in a superclass of
`MountTable`. What is visible, however, is the static method `getMountPoint()`,
which takes a device number and returns the corresponding mountpoint. Another method, `getTableSize()`, tells the number of available physical devices
(which can be different for different parameter files). Device numbers range
from 0 to `getTableSize()-1`. Thus, together these methods make it possible
to access all mountpoints. To provide the file-to-device mapping, the student
needs to implement the following methods of class `MountTable`:

⋄ `public static boolean do_isMountPoint(String dirname)`
  This method tells if `dirname` is a mountpoint of one of the devices. It uses
  the method `getMountPoint()` internally.

⋄ `public static int do_getDeviceID(String pathname)`
  This method checks the mount table and returns the Id of the device that
  hosts the file with the given `pathname`. The method for determining the
  device was described earlier.

As you can see, there are no methods for creating or deleting mountpoints.
In *OSP 2* all mountpoints are created by the system at startup and none gets
destroyed during the execution of the system.

Built-ins and relevant methods from other classes.   The implementation of these methods might need to use the following methods:

⋄ `public static String getMountPoint(int deviceID)`   MountTable
  Returns the mountpoint associated with device `deviceID`. This method
  is an *OSP 2* built-in.

⋄ `public static int getDeviceID(String pathname)`   MountTable
  Returns the device Id that hosts `pathname`. Note that this method eventually calls your method `do_getDeviceID()` described above. You have
  to use `getDeviceID()` here instead of `do_getDeviceID()` because of
  the convention explained in Section 1.9.2 that prohibits student modules from calling the `do_` methods.

⋄ `final static public int getTableSize()`   Device
Tells how many devices there are. The number of devices is specified in
the parameter file and can vary from one simulation run to another.

⋄ `final static public Device get(int deviceID)`   Device
Returns the device object with the given Id. In conjunction with
`getTableSize()`, this method can be used in a loop to examine each
device in turn, as device IDs range from 0 to `getTableSize()-1`. Note
that all devices are mounted by $\mathcal{OSP}\,2$ at the beginning of the simulation and no devices are added or removed during a simulation run.
Therefore the number of devices remains constant and the device table
has no "holes".

Summary of the class `MountTable`

This class maintains the mount table data structure, which maintains the correspondence between devices and directories through which these devices are
accessed by the programs. Other modules of the file system layer access the
mount table mainly using the methods `getMountPoint()` and `getDeviceID()`.

7.5 Class `INode`

An $\mathcal{OSP}\,2$ inode represents a concrete file. An inode records information about
the device where the file lives, and it keeps track of the blocks occupied by the
file, the hard link count, and the open count.

The most important information here is the set of blocks occupied by the
file. The actual data structure to be used to capture this information is up to
the student implementation, although the course instructor may have specific
requirements for this data structure.

The following methods of class `INode` are to be implemented as part of the
FILESYS project:

⋄ `public INode(int deviceID)`
The constructor. It should call `super(deviceID)` and then initialize the instance variables of the inode (if necessary).

⋄ `public static boolean do_isFreeBlock(int block, int deviceID)`
Tells whether `block` on device with Id `deviceID` is free.[3]

---

[3] Note that from an object-oriented design perspective, this method better fits in
class `Device`. However, space management is not a function of the basic I/O su-

⋄ `public int do_allocateFreeBlock()`
When applied to an inode object, allocates a free block to that inode and returns the block number of that block. Marks the block as used. Make sure that the INode block count is set correctly (see the method `setBlockCount()`). Returns NONE if the device has no free blocks.

⋄ `public void do_releaseBlocks()`
Releases all disk blocks occupied by the inode. Make sure that the INode block count is set correctly (`setBlockCount()`).

It is clear from the above that you have to keep track of the free space on the device. For some representations, such as bitmaps, it is useful to know the size of each device in blocks. The size can be obtained using the method `getNumberOfBlocks()` of the class `Device`.

Since you have to keep track of the valid inodes, you might also need to implement the **file allocation table** (or a **master file table**) thats hold these inodes.

Relevant methods defined in other classes.

⋄ `final public int getNumberOfBlocks()`   Device
Returns the total number of blocks on the device.

⋄ `final static public int getTableSize()`   Device
Returns the total number of devices in the device table (i.e., in the current simulation of the $\mathcal{OSP}\,2$ system).

⋄ `public final int getBlockCount()`   INode
Returns the number of blocks allocated to this inode. This method is inherited from a superclass of INode.

⋄ `public final void setBlockCount(int blockCount)`   INode
Sets the number of blocks allocated to this inode. This method is inherited from a superclass.

⋄ `public final int getDeviceID()`   INode
Returns the device ID of this inode.

⋄ `public static String getMountPoint(int deviceID)`   MountTable
Returns the mountpoint of the given device.

_____

pervisor that `Device` implements. This is an example of the tension between the layered architecture of an OS and the object-oriented design.

Summary of the class `INode`

The `INode` class has methods (implemented as built-ins) and variables which provide access to the various components of that class, as listed below:

openCount: The count of active open-file handles associated with the inode, obtained using `getOpenCount()` and changed via `incrementOpenCount()` and `decrementOpenCount()`.

hardLinkCount: The number of pathnames associated with the inode. This count is obtained via `getLinkCount()` and changed using the methods `incrementLinkCount()` and `decrementLinkCount()`.

blockCount: The number of blocks allocated to the file (the file size). This item is obtained using `getBlockCount()` and set using `setBlockCount()`.

device ID: The device Id of the inode. It can be obtained using the method `getDeviceID()`.

7.6 Class `DirectoryEntry`

If you were wondering how pathnames are associated with inodes, the suspense is over: this is done through directory entries defined by the class `Directory-Entry`. A directory entry includes a pathname, an inode, and a type (`FileEntry` or `DirEntry`). The type indicates whether the particular directory entry represents a plain file or a directory.

The methods of this class to be implemented as part of the FILESYS project are listed below.

◇ `public DirectoryEntry(String pathname, int type, INode inode)`
The class constructor. Calls `super()`, as usual, and initializes instance variables, if necessary.

◇ `public static INode do_getINodeOf(String pathname)`
Given a pathname, returns the corresponding inode. In order to make this possible, the class `DirectoryEntry` must maintain the collection of all directory entries.

In addition, you need to implement a number of supporting methods that other classes in your package might need to use to insert directory entries into the directories, delete the entries, etc.

Relevant builtins and methods defined in other classes.   This class does not use any standard methods defined in other classes of $\mathcal{OSP}$ 2. Some standard classes provided by Java itself might be useful. For instance, `Hashtable` and the associated methods can be used to maintain the `Directory-Entry` data structure. This would closely correspond to how directories are implemented in real operating systems.

Summary of Class `DirectoryEntry`

This class does not provide any methods, but there are several variables:

pathname: This property is accessible through the method

```
final public String getPathname()
```

This is the pathname represented by this directory entry.

INode: This property is accessible through the method

```
final public INode getINode()
```

It is the inode that this directory entry associates with the pathname of the directory entry. A related method in this class is `getINodeOf()`, which takes a pathname parameter and returns the corresponding INode:

```
final public static INode getINodeOf(String pathname)
```

Unlike `getINode()`, this method is static.

type: This property is accessible through the method

```
final public int getType()
```

It specifies the type of the directory entry, i.e., whether the entry represents a regular plain file (`FileEntry`) or a directory (`DirEntry`).

7.7 Class OpenFile

Class OpenFile provides methods for creating open-file handles, accessing the components of an open-file handle, and using open-file handles to perform I/O operations.

⋄ public OpenFile(INode inode, TaskCB task)
This is a constructor for open-file handles. It must call super() with the same set of parameters and then, possibly, initialize the various variables that you might have added to the class.

⋄ static public OpenFile do_open(String filename, TaskCB task)
This method create an open-file handle. It receives a file name (which must correspond to a previously created file) and a task object, creates an open-file handle for the file, and adds the handle to the task's table of open files. (Recall from Chapter 3 that the open-files table is one of the resources owned by a task.)

First, the file must already exist before it can be opened. Existence should be checked using a method that you implement in class FileSys. Note that this method will be unknown to the $\mathcal{OSP}$ 2 IFL layer, i.e. it will not have a wrapper method in the IFL, and therefore its implementation and name are completely up to you. Second, opening a mountpoint is a violation, so you must check that the argument is not a mountpoint. (The method isMountPoint() of class MountTable can be used to check this.)

Once you pass these checks, a new open-file handle can be created. The OpenFile() constructor takes an inode and a task as parameters, so you must obtain the inode corresponding to filename (using the method getINodeOf() discussed earlier). After constructing the handle, you should add it to the task with the method addFile() of class TaskCB. Finally, the count of open files for the inode should be incremented (incrementOpenCount()) and the newly created file handle returned.

⋄ public int do_close()
A file is closed when its open-file handle is no longer needed. However, closing a file is trickier than it might seem.

First, the file might still have outstanding (unprocessed) IORBs. As discussed in Chapter 6, such a file cannot be closed immediately. Instead, you should *mark* the file as needing to be closed later and leave it alone. Marking is performed by setting the closePending flag to true, where closePending is a field of the context OpenFile object. The disk interrupt handler will close the file (by issuing another close operation) after the last outstanding IORB has been processed.

If the file *cannot* be closed due to outstanding IORBs, as described above, do_close() should just exit and return FAILURE. If the file *can* be closed immediately, then you should do so, adjusting the relevant structures. One thing that needs to be done here is to decrement the open file count of the inode associated with the file handle. The inode is obtained using the getINode() method and the count is changed using decrementOpenCount() of class INode.

Next, you should check whether you can destroy the inode associated with the file handle and release the disk blocks owned by that inode. As discussed earlier, an inode can be deleted when both its open file count (getOpenCount()) and its hard-link count (getLinkCount()) are zero. The inode's disk blocks are released with the method releaseBlocks() of class INode. The method to remove an inode from the disk master file table should reside in class INode and its name (and, of course, its implementation) are left for you to decide.

Finally, the closePending field is reset to false, the file handle is removed from the open-files table of the task associated with that handle, and SUCCESS is returned.

◇ public int do_read(int fileBlockNumber,
   PageTableEntry memoryPage, ThreadCB thread)
The do_read() method is executed on a file-handle object. It creates a read request to the device associated with the file handle, enqueues the request to the device, and waits until the I/O is complete — I/O operations in $OSP\ 2$ are synchronous at the thread level. That is, the thread that issues an I/O operation is eventually blocked until the operation is finished.[4]

It is recommended that you make sure that the parameters passed to open() are consistent. For example, the fileBlockNumber parameter must be within the appropriate range (non-negative and not exceed the file size). If it is not, FAILURE should be returned. Likewise, it is wise to check whether memoryPage and thread are not null.

In the next step, a new system event is created using the constructor SystemEvent() and the current thread is suspended on that event. At this point it is recommended that you refresh your memory about thread suspension and resumption by (re-)reading Section 4.3. A thread that is suspended on a system event is not really blocked, but instead can be thought of as

---

[4] However, I/O is asynchronous at the task level: a thread that does not wish to wait for I/O can spawn another thread that performs the I/O. Meanwhile, the first thread can go about its business while the second thread would wait. When the I/O is done, the two threads can merge.

having changed status from user thread to system thread. When the read operation is complete, the event will "happen" and the thread will be resumed. To be able to resume the thread after the I/O is complete, you should save the **SystemEvent** object in a variable.

You are now ready to construct an IORB for the request. The inode and device Id can be extracted from the open-file handle using the appropriate methods. The I/O type (one of the parameters in the IORB constructor) is, naturally, **FileRead**. The only thing that requires care is the disk block number parameter to the constructor.

Note that the **fileBlockNumber** parameter to **do_read()** is the number of the *logical* block within a file. It must be mapped to the *physical* block of the disk. Information about the disk blocks allocated to the file is stored in the inode, which is implemented in your **INode** class. It is recommended that you implement a method in **INode** that, when applied to an inode with a logical file block number as a parameter, returns the corresponding physical block.

After collecting all the needed components, you use the **IORB()** constructor to create an IORB for the read request.

Next, you must enqueue the request to the appropriate device using the method **enqueueIORB()** of class **Device**. Note that **enqueueIORB()** locks the target memory buffer page, which can cause some swapping activity, and the thread must wait until swapping is finished. As usual in $\mathcal{OSP}\,2$, a waiting thread might get killed, so it is necessary to ascertain that the thread is still alive after **enqueueIORB()** returns. If the thread was killed, **do_read()** should return **FAILURE**.

If **enqueueIORB()** finished successfully, **thread** must be suspended on **iorb**. When this I/O completes, **thread** will be notified and control will get past the **suspend()** operation. At this point, again, you must check if the thread is still alive. If it is dead, **FAILURE** is returned; if it is alive, you execute **notifyThreads()** on the previously created **SystemEvent** object and return SUCCESS.[5]

⋄ public int do_write(int fileBlockNumber,
PageTableEntry memoryPage, ThreadCB thread)

Writing is similar to reading in many respects. One important difference (in $\mathcal{OSP}\,2$, anyway) is that a file block is considered out of range only if it is

---

[5] Note that the logic of your implementation should be such that each **suspend()** is matched by a **notifyThreads()** system call.

negative. If `fileBlockNumber` is higher than the number of blocks in the file, the file is extended with the necessary number of blocks. For example, if the current size of the file is 2 blocks and `fileBlockNumber` is 5, then 4 new blocks must be allocated to the file. (Note that blocks are counted from 0, so 5 refers to the 6th block of the file.) Additional disk blocks are allocated to an inode as a result of the `allocateFreeBlock()` system call (*and not by any other means!*).

Another important difference is that the device might not have enough free space to accommodate the file expansion. In this case, `FAILURE` should be returned. Note that free disk space management is done in class `INode` and is the student's responsibility.

Relevant methods defined in other classes.

◇ `public static boolean isMountPoint(String dir)`   MountTable
  Tells if `dir` is a mountpoint.

◇ `final public void addFile(OpenFile file)`   TaskCB
  Adds `file` to the open-files table of the task.

◇ `final public void removeFile(OpenFile file)`   TaskCB
  Removes the file handle from the task's open files table.

◇ `final public void suspend(Event event)`   ThreadCB
  Suspends thread on the event.

◇ `public void notifyThreads()`   Event
  Notifies threads that are waiting on the event.

◇ `final public int getIORBCount()`   OpenFile
  Returns the IORB count of the open-file handle.

◇ `final public void incrementIORBCount()`   OpenFile
  Increments the IORB count of the open-file handle by 1.

◇ `final public void decrementIORBCount()`   OpenFile
  Decrements the IORB count of the open-file handle by 1.

◇ `final public INode getINode()`   OpenFile
  Returns the inode of the open-file handle.

◇ `final public void setINode(INode inode)`   OpenFile
  Sets the inode of the open file handle.

◇ `final public TaskCB getTask()`   OpenFile
  Returns the task of the open-file handle.

⋄ public final int getOpenCount()   INode
Returns the open file count of inode.

⋄ public final void incrementOpenCount()   INode
Increments the open-file count of the inode by 1.

⋄ public final void decrementOpenCount()   INode
Decrements the open file count of inode by 1.

⋄ final public void releaseBlocks()   INode
Frees up disk blocks held by the inode.

⋄ public SystemEvent(String type)   SystemEvent
The constructor for system events. The type parameter is used to provide a tag with which the event will be displayed in the log file. This
tag can be useful for debugging when you need to trace the execution
of your project. When a thread is suspended on a SystemEvent, it can
be thought of as having changed status from user thread to system
thread. See Section 4.3 for more details on suspension and resumption
of threads.

⋄ public IORB(ThreadCB thread, PageTableEntry page,
int blockNumber, int deviceID, int ioType, OpenFile openFile)
Creates an IORB with the given parameters.

⋄ final public int enqueueIORB(IORB iorb)   Device
Enqueues iorb to its associated device. This operation is blocking and can cause a pagefault (and the ensuing swapping) because
enqueueIORB() needs to lock the target memory page in order to shield
it from page replacement. See Chapters 5 and 6 for a more thorough
explanation of page locking. This method returns SUCCESS if iorb has
been successfully enqueued. A failure is returned when enqueuing fails
(for example, if the original thread has died).

⋄ final public int allocateFreeBlock()   INode
Allocates a free block to the inode. The block becomes occupied.

Summary of the class OpenFile

The class OpenFile maintains the following important variables, which are
affected using the various methods of that class.

IORB count: The number of outstanding IORBs for the handle. Obtained
using getIORBCount() and changed using incrementIORBCount() and
decrementIORBCount().

INode: The inode of the open-file handle. Obtained using getINode() and set using setINode().

Task: The task that owns the open-file handle. Obtained using the getTask() method.

closePending: This field is set to true by do_close() if the OpenFile object has outstanding IORBs and cannot be closed immediately. When the last IORB for this OpenFile object is processed, do_close() will close the file.

7.8 Class FileSys

You are to implement the following methods of class FileSys as part of this project.

◇ public static void init()
As usual in $\mathcal{OSP}$ 2, this method is called at the beginning of every simulation run. It can be used to initialize static variables that your implementation might use (for example, the variables used in the implementation of the mount table, in the open-files table, in the list of free blocks on the various devices, etc.).

◇ final static public int do_create(String pathname, int size)
This method creates a file with a given pathname and size (in bytes). In one sentence, this means making the necessary checks and then creating the corresponding inode and the directory entry that relates pathname with that inode. The devil is in the details, however, and this is what we will be discussing next.

First, you have to check if the file with the same name already exists. If so, FAILURE is returned. If a file is a mountpoint (is listed in the mount table), then it is presumed to exist right from the start and, since mountpoints cannot be created or destroyed, FAILURE should be returned in this case as well. If the file does not exist, check if pathname refers to a directory or a plain file. A pathname refers to a directory if it ends with the filename separator, DirSeparator, but is not a mountpoint. It refers to a plain file otherwise.

Note, however, that the convention that a directory name must end with DirSeparator is used in the create() call only (just in order to avoid introducing yet another system call). In all other contexts, pathnames such as /foo/bar and /foo/bar/ refer to the same directory. Also, if a plain file by the name /foo/bar already exists and do_create() is called with

/foo/bar/ as a parameter, the call should fail and FAILURE returned, because there *cannot* be a file and a directory with the same name. Likewise, if do_create("/foo/bar/",...) was earlier called to create a directory, then a subsequent call do_create("/foo/bar",...) should fail, because otherwise we would have a file and a directory with the same name.

In view of the above, it is generally a good idea to **normalize** file names before doing any file-name comparisons. A **normalized pathname** is a full pathname such that it does not have repeated occurrences of DirSeparator (pathnames /foo///bar// and /foo/bar/ are considered the same, but only the latter is normalized). It may be convenient to also remove the trailing DirSeparator in normalized directory names (except for the root of the file system, /), but this depends on the particular algorithms that you are using.

Next, you must check if the caller intended to create a file or a directory by checking the last character of pathname. The appropriate file-type indicator (FileEntry or DirEntry) will later go into the directory entry for the file. Also, for plain files, the size parameter indicates the size of the file in bytes. However, for directories this parameter is ignored, since directories are assumed to occupy *exactly one* disk block. The correct size parameter should be used when constructing the corresponding inode.

It is common in programming to attempt to create a file in a non-existent directory with the intent that the system would create all the intermediate subdirectories automatically. For instance, suppose that the directory /foo exists, but /foo/bar does not. In *OSP 2*, the call do_create("/foo/bar/moo/abc.html",...) should then create the intermediate directories, /foo/bar and /foo/bar/moo, before creating /foo/bar/moo/abc.html. Note that this means that while creating the intermediate directories, do_create() will call create() (its *OSP 2* wrapper), which in turn will call do_create() *recursively*.

Next you should check the mount table to determine the device where the file is to be created. Recall from Section 7.4 that determining the device is the job of method getDeviceID() of class MountTable. You need to make sure that the device has enough free space. Recall that space management is the job of the INode class. You might want to implement a method in that class which returns the number of free blocks. If this number is less than the number of blocks needed to accommodate our file, FAILURE should be returned. It is therefore important to correctly calculate the number of blocks needed to accommodate a file-creation request. Recall that do_create() gets the size of the file in bytes, and this has to be converted into disk blocks. The block size equals the size of a virtual memory page, which can be obtained using the two methods provided by the class MMU: getVirtualAddressBits() and getPageAddressBits().[6]

Note, however, that $\mathcal{OSP}$ 2 assumes that directories occupy exactly one block and the file-size parameter in do_create() should be ignored in this case.

After all these checks, nothing (but a computer crash) can stop us from creating the file. You can use the constructor for the class INode to create a new inode. Next, you should use methods incrementLinkCount() and allocateFreeBlock() of INode to update the count of hard links to the inode and to allocate the right number of disk blocks to it. The inode should also be inserted into the device's file allocation table for safekeeping.

To complete the process, you must create a directory entry for pathname and insert it into the appropriate directory. This is accomplished using the constructor of DirectoryEntry and other methods that depend on your implementation of directories.

When all is done, SUCCESS is returned.

◇ final static public int do_link(String pathname, String linkname)

This method creates a new hard link, with name linkname, to the inode associated with pathname. The process is similar to creating a file: you need to check if a directory entry for linkname already exists and return FAILURE if it does. Otherwise (if there is no file named linkname), you must create an appropriate directory entry. However, there also are significant differences between linking and creating files.

First, no new inode need be created. Instead, the inode associated with pathname is used. Therefore, no additional space need be allocated. Second, hard links to directories are not allowed (as in Unix). Third, unlike the case of file creation, no intermediate directories are created. So, if the directory /foo exists but /foo/bar does not, then creation of a hard link /foo/bar/abc.html to another file should fail.

Other than that, creation of a new directory entry to associate linkname with the inode of pathname proceeds as in the case of do_create(). In particular, do not forget to increment the hard-link count.

Note one interesting thing: after a hard link to an inode is created, linkname and pathname become virtually indistinguishable. That is, linkname is as much of a "file name" for the corresponding inode as pathname is. The inode

---

[6] Note that a file-creation request might specify size 0, in which case the request must succeed even if the device has no room.

itself does not contain any file-name information and all the naming takes place in directory entries.

⋄ **final static public int do_delete(String pathname)**
Destroying a file is not as simple as it might seem. First, you must check if a file with the name **pathname** exists. Note that you cannot always tell from the name whether it refers to a plain file or a directory, so you must use normalized names to do the checks. Also, non-empty directories cannot be deleted and, of course, deletion of mountpoints is not allowed. In all these cases, **FAILURE** should be returned.

Once you get past these checks, you must remember that **pathname** is just one of the several possible hard links to the inode associated with a file. If after deleting the directory entry for **pathname** and decrementing the hard-link count the number of hard links for the inode (obtained via **getLinkCount()**) is non-zero, do not delete the inode. Recall that inodes also have an open count, in addition to a hard-link count, which counts the number of open-file handles for the inode. If this count is positive, the inode must *not* be deleted. In both cases, however, the directory entry for **pathname** must still be deleted. If the hard-link count as well as the open count are zero, both the inode and the directory entry must be deleted. In case the inode is deleted, all its blocks must be freed up (using **releaseBlocks()**). Finally, **SUCCESS** should be returned.

⋄ **final static public Vector do_dir(String dirname)**
This method returns a vector of *normalized* file names that reside in directory **dirname**. If **dirname** does not exist or is not a directory, **null** is returned.

Relevant methods from other classes. The following methods might be required to implement class **FileSys**.

⋄ **public static boolean isMountPoint(String dir)**   MountTable
Tells if a given pathname is a mountpoint.

⋄ **static final public int getVirtualAddressBits()**   MMU
Tells how many bits are used to represent a virtual address. This method and the next method can be used to determine how many bits are needed to represent an address within a page, from which the page/block size can be computed.

⋄ **static final public int getPageAddressBits()**   MMU
Tells the number of bits used to represent a page address.

⋄ **public final int getLinkCount()**   INode
Returns the number of hard links to the inode.

◇ `public final void decrementLinkCount()`   INode
Decrements the hard-link count for inode.

◇ `public final void incrementLinkCount()`   INode
Increments the hard-link count for the inode.

◇ `public final int getOpenCount()`   INode
Returns the count of open-file handles for the inode.

◇ `final public int allocateFreeBlock()`   INode
Allocates a free block to the inode. The block becomes occupied.

◇ `final public void releaseBlocks()`   INode
Releases all the blocks held by the inode.

◇ `public final int getDeviceID()`   INode
Tells the device Id of the inode.

◇ `final public static int create(String name, int size)`   FileSys
The $\mathcal{OSP}$ 2 wrapper for `do_create()`

◇ `final public static INode getINodeOf(String pathname)`
                                                     DirectoryEntry
Returns the inode associated with **pathname**. If no directory entry for **pathname** exists, returns **null**.

◇ `final public static void showDirectory(String dirname)`
                                                     DirectoryEntry
Prints the directory listing for **dirname** to the log file. This
method can be useful for debugging, since it shows what
$\mathcal{OSP}$ 2 believes the correct listing is supposed to be.

Summary of Class FileSys

In $\mathcal{OSP}$ 2, the class **FileSys** does not typically maintain important data structures of its own. Instead, it serves as a container for methods that do not
logically belong to any other class in the package. For instance, the method
`do_delete()` for deleting files based on a string that represents the file name
cannot be naturally attached to any other $\mathcal{OSP}$ 2 class. Such methods do not
normally maintain complex data of its own. Instead, they operate on the data
structures defined in other classes, such as **DirectoryEntry** or **MountTable**,
using the methods provided in those classes.

7.9 Methods Exported by the FILESYS Package

The following is a summary of the public methods defined in the classes of the FILESYS package or in the corresponding superclasses, which can be used to implement this and other student packages. To the right of each method we list the class of objects to which the method applies.

◇ `final public static int create(String name, int size)`   FileSys
    Creates a file with the specified name and size.

◇ `final public static void delete(String name)`   FileSys
    Deletes the directory entry for the specified file.

◇ `final public static OpenFile open(String filename, TaskCB task)`
    OpenFile
    Opens the specified file `filename` by `task` and returns the newly created open-file handle (or `null`, if the operation fails).

◇ `final public int close()`   OpenFile
    Closes the file handle on which this operation is invoked.

◇ `final public void read(int fileBlockNumber,`   OpenFile
    `PageTableEntry memoryPage, ThreadCB thread)`
    Performs the read I/O operation using the given open-file handle. Reads data from logical file block `fileBlockNumber` into `memoryPage` on behalf of `thread`.

◇ `final public void write(int fileBlockNumber,`   OpenFile
    `PageTableEntry memoryPage, ThreadCB thread)`
    Performs the write I/O operation using the given open-file handle. Writes data to logical file block `fileBlockNumber` from `memoryPage` on behalf of `thread`.

PORTS: *Interprocess Communication*

8.1 Chapter Objective

The objective of the PORTS project is to teach students about interprocess communication and requires that the student implement two public classes: `Message`, which describes what $\mathcal{OSP}\,2$ messages look like, and `PortCB`, which implements the main communication primitives, such as `send()` and `receive()`.

8.2 Interprocess Communication in $\mathcal{OSP}\,2$

Interprocess communication in $\mathcal{OSP}\,2$ is based on the abstraction of a **port** and is modeled after the Mach micro-kernel. In Mach, a process can open a port, and other processes can then send messages to it which can be received by the owning process; a message is basically a block of bytes. Mach manages the ports, and provides guaranteed, in-order delivery, with large messages being handled efficiently by sharing pages between address spaces. There is a sophisticated permission mechanism which restricts the operations that processes can perform on ports.

Thus, a port is like your home mailbox. A task can create a port to serve as a mailbox to which threads from other tasks can send messages.[1] Only threads

---

[1] Note that threads of the same task do not need to communicate this way, since

of the owner task can read from the ports of that task; other threads only write to that port. In *OSP 2*, reading from a port is done using the `receive()` operation and writing is performed via the `send()` operation.

The *OSP 2* model of communication is based on *reliable* message delivery, i.e., correctly formed messages never get lost. When threads communicate, they exchange discrete entities, called **messages**. A message has length and Id. When a thread sends a message to a port, the message is delivered to the destination port and is placed in that port's **message buffer**. Port buffers are assumed to have finite byte size specified in a global constant `PortBufferLength`. If the message is bigger than this amount, the `send()` operation fails and the message is not delivered. If the message is smaller than `PortBufferLength`, it is considered well-formed and deliverable. However, the destination port might not have enough room due to other messages that might have been delivered to that port but not yet consumed. In this case, the `send()` operation suspends the sender thread until room becomes available.

When a thread wants to receive a message, it invokes the `receive()` method on a port. If a message is available, it is removed from the port message buffer and the operation succeeds. If, however, the port is empty, then the receiver thread is suspended until a message arrives.

It is thus clear that a mechanism is needed for threads to suspend themselves and to be notified. In *OSP 2*, this is accomplished through the familiar `Event` class. More precisely, `PortCB` is a subclass of `Event`, and threads can suspend themselves on a port when necessary. Likewise, when appropriate conditions arise (e.g., a port buffer gets more room or a message arrives at an empty port), threads that are waiting on the port can be notified. (Note that several threads can be waiting on the same port at the same time.)

The classes comprising the PORTS package are described below. The class diagram of Figure 8.1 places these classes in the overall context of the *OSP 2* system.

8.3 The Message Class

The `Message` class has only one required method, the class constructor, which takes a `length` argument and creates a message with a unique Id.

⋄ `public Message(int length)`

The message constructor. Must call `super(length)` as its first statement. Your implementation might also add other fields and methods to this class.

_____

they share virtual address space and thus can communicate much more efficiently through shared variables.

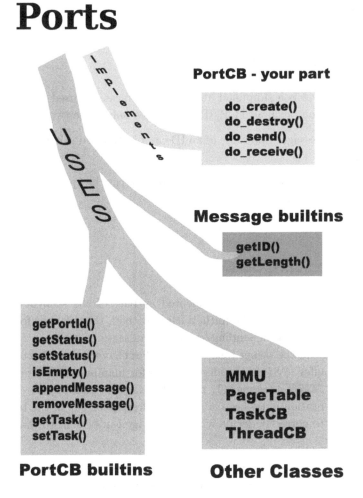

Figure 8.1 A diagram summarizing the package PORTS.

In addition, your implementation of class `PortCB` can use a number of methods defined in class `Message` provided by $\mathcal{OSP}$ *2*:

◇ `public int getID()`
   Returns the Id of the message.

◇ `public int getLength()`
   Returns the length of the message in bytes.

Built-ins and relevant methods defined in other classes. The method constructor for class Message does not use any methods provided by other $\mathcal{OSP}$ 2 classes.

Summary of Class Message

A message in $\mathcal{OSP}$ 2 is a simplified abstraction of messages used in real communication protocols, such as TCP/IP: it includes only these two parameters:

ID: The ID of a message. The value of an ID can be retrieved using the method getID().

length: The length of a message. This parameter can be queried using the method getLength().

8.4 The PortCB Class

The methods of PortCB to be implemented as part of the student project include the class constructor, the initialization method, the methods for creating/destroying ports and for sending/receiving messages.

A port has an Id, the owner task, a status (PortLive or PortDestroyed), and a message buffer. $\mathcal{OSP}$ 2 provides methods for manipulating the message buffer of a port (appendMessage(), removeMessage(), isEmpty()), but the student implementation must keep track of the free space left in the buffer in order to be able to correctly decide when a message can be sent to the port.

◇ public PortCB()
This is a class constructor whose only required statement is super(), the usual call to the corresponding constructor in the superclass.

◇ public static void init()
This is the usual initialization method, which is called at the very beginning of the simulation run. It is a place where your implementation can initialize static variables.

◇ public static PortCB do_create()
This method creates and returns a new port. After a new PortCB object is created, it needs to be assigned to the current task, i.e., the task that owns the currently running thread. Recall from Chapter 5 that PTBR, the page table base register, always points to the page table of the current

task. Thus, the current task can be retrieved using the following idiom:
`MMU.getPTBR().getTask()`.

To assign the port to the task, use the method `addPort()` of `TaskCB`. However, keep in mind that there is a limit of how many ports a task can have, which is defined by the global constant `MaxPortsPerTask`. If the task already has that many ports, `addPort()` will return `FAILURE` and `do_create()` should then return the `null` object.

If all is well, the owner task of the port should be set (using `setTask()`), and the status set to `PortLive` using the method `setStatus()` of class `PortCB`, which is provided by *OSP 2*. In addition, you have to initialize the variables that you might have introduced to keep track of the state of the message buffer. Finally, the newly created `PortCB` object is returned.

◇ `public void do_destroy()`
 Ports are destroyed by the owner task when they are no longer needed for the task's operation or when the task itself is killed. To destroy a port, the port's status should be set to `PortDestroyed`, and the port should be removed from the task's table of active ports. The latter is accomplished using the method `removePort()` of `TaskCB`. Next, the port's owner task should be set to null using the method `setTask()` of `PortCB`.

You must also notify the threads that might be waiting for an event associated with this port. As usual, this is accomplished using the method `notifyThreads()` applied to the appropriate event.

◇ `public int do_send(Message msg)`
 Prior to sending a message, you must first check that the message is well-formed. In *OSP 2*, this means that the parameter `msg` is not `null` and that the message length is not greater than the length of the port message buffer. If the message is not well-formed, `FAILURE` should be returned.

In the next step, a new system event must be created using the constructor `SystemEvent()` and the current thread must be suspended on that event. You already saw how to find the current task from the page table base register. The current thread is obtained using the method `getCurrentThread()` of that task.

At this point it is recommended that you refresh your memory about thread suspension and resumption as described in Section 4.3. A thread that is suspended on a system event is not really blocked, but instead can be thought of as having changed status from user thread to system thread. When the send operation is complete, the event will "happen" and the thread will be resumed. To be able to resume the thread before leaving `do_send()`, you should save the `SystemEvent` object in a variable.

Now you are ready to attempt to send the message. Recall that if the destination port (i.e., the port on which the `send()` method is executed) does not have enough room in the message buffer, the sender thread must be suspended on that port. (Recall that you have saved the information about that thread before suspending it on a `SystemEvent`.) A thread T suspended on a port can be woken up when the port gets more room in its buffer. This happens when one of the threads that owns the port executes a `receive()` operation on that port. However, the sending thread T might discover that the port still does not have enough room for the message because either too little space was freed up or because some other thread managed to send a message to the port before T had a chance. In this case, T has to be suspended again (on the same port).

Another possibility is that the newly awakened thread was killed while waiting to send the message. `FAILURE` should be returned in this case. The third possibility is that the thread might have been awakened because the owner task decided to destroy the port on which the thread was suspended (or, maybe, the task itself was killed). Again, `FAILURE` should be returned. In addition, you should notify the threads that were suspended on the `SystemEvent` associated with the current send operation. (Recall that the current thread was suspended on this event at the beginning of the `do_send()` method.)

If none of the above problems are detected, you know that send should succeed. Thus, you should update the message buffer of the port (using `appendMessage()`) and, if the buffer was previously empty, notify the threads that may be waiting on that port in the receive mode.[2] Finally, you should execute `notifyThreads()` on the previously created `SystemEvent` object and return SUCCESS.

◇ `public Message do_receive()`

First, you must check that the receive operation is permitted, i.e., that the receiving thread's task owns the port on which `do_receive()` has been invoked. If this is not the case, `null` should be returned. Second, when a thread T executes a `receive()` operation on a port P, you must create a `SystemEvent` object and suspend T on that event. As explained earlier, this corresponds to T changing its status from user thread to system thread. Note that the receiving thread T is the currently executing thread, which can be obtained using the PTBR.

---

[2] Note that other threads may have been waiting to receive a message from this port *only* if its message buffer was empty.

Next, recall that the receiving thread must be suspended if the message buffer of the port contains no messages. This thread can be woken up when some other thread sends a message to that port. However, keep in mind that although a port can have several threads suspended in receive mode, only one of them will be awakened and thereby succeed in getting a message. All other threads would have to be suspended again.

There is a possibility that a woken-up thread was killed or that the port was destroyed. In both cases, do_receive must return the null object. If none of the above bad things happen, the do_receive() method succeeds. In this case, the method should "consume" a message from the port message buffer using removeMessage() and notify threads waiting on the port. (This is needed because consuming a message will probably free up space in the message buffer of the port and, as a result, some previously suspended send operation might be able to proceed.) Finally, the message consumed by this receive operation should be returned.

In all cases (whether the receive operation ended successfully or not), prior to exiting you must execute notifyThreads() on the previously created SystemEvent object for this receive operation.

Built-ins and relevant methods from other classes. A typical implementation of the methods in class PortCB uses the following methods defined in other classes or methods of PortCB provided by $\mathcal{OSP}$ 2:

◇ final public int addPort(PortCB newPort)   TaskCB
Adds a new port to the task.

◇ public int removePort(PortCB oldPort)
Removes oldPort from the task.

◇ public ThreadCB getCurrentThread()   TaskCB
Returns the currently running thread of the task. Null, if the task itself is not current.

◇ static public PageTable getPTBR()   MMU
Returns the value of PTBR.

◇ public final TaskCB getTask()   PageTable
Returns the owner task for the page table.

◇ final public int getStatus()   ThreadCB
Tells the status of the thread.

◇ final public void suspend(Event event)   ThreadCB
Suspends the thread on event.

◇ `final public int getStatus()`   PortCB
    Tells the status of the port.

◇ `final public void setStatus()`   PortCB
    Sets the status of the port.

◇ `final public void setTask(TaskCB owner)`   PortCB
    Sets the port owner.

◇ `final public TaskCB getTask()`   PortCB
    Tells who owns the port.

◇ `final public Message removeMessage()`   PortCB
    Removes a message from the port's message buffer.

◇ `final public void appendMessage(Message msg)`   PortCB
    Appends a new message to the port's message buffer.

◇ `final public boolean isEmpty()`   PortCB
    Checks if the port's message buffer is empty.

Summary of the `PortCB` class

The `PortCB` class maintains information about the open ports attached to the various processes. The following list describes the main attributes of a port and the methods that are used to query these attributes.

Port ID: $\mathcal{OSP}$ 2 assigns an ID to each port at creation time. This ID can be retrieved using the method `getPortID()` of the `PortCB` class.

Owner: This is the task that owns the port. This attribute is manipulated using the methods `getTask()` and `setTask()`.

Status: `PortLive` or `PortDestroyed`. This attribute is manipulated using the methods `getStatus()` and `setStatus()`.

Message buffer: This buffer is manipulated using the methods `appendMessage()`, `removeMessage()`, and `isEmpty()` of class `PortCB`, and are provided by $\mathcal{OSP}$ 2. However, your implementation must keep track of the free space left in the message buffer.

8.5 Methods Exported by Package PORTS

The PORTS package exports the following methods that are used by other packages in the system:

◇ `final static public void create()`
Creates a new port.

◇ `final public void destroy()`
Destroys an existing port.

◇ `final public void send(Message msg)`
Sends a message, `msg`, to the port on which this method is invoked.

◇ `final public Message receive()`
Receives a message from the port on which this method is invoked.

9

RESOURCES: *Resource Management*

9.1 Chapter Objective

The objective of the RESOURCES project is to expose students to the concept of shared resources in a concurrent system, and to provide an environment in which they can implement various deadlock-handling techniques. $\mathcal{OSP}$ 2 simulation supports two approaches to handling deadlock in an operating system: **deadlock avoidance** and **deadlock detection**, discussed further below. To this end, students will be asked to implement the three public classes of the RESOURCES package: `ResourceCB`, the resource control block; `RRB`, the resource request block; and `ResourceTable`.

9.2 Overview of Resource Management

The RESOURCES project focuses on techniques for managing shared resources in a concurrent system. Examples of such resources include files, printer, disks, and interprocess-communication messaging buffer space. When processes compete for access to shared resources, especially when such access is exclusive, deadlock becomes an issue. Simply put, deadlock arises when there exists a closed chain of processes such that each process holds at least one resource needed by the next process in the chain. This phenomenon is known as **circular wait**.

For circular wait to exist it must be the case that processes require:

Mutual Exclusion. Mutually exclusive access to resources;

Hold and Wait. A process may hold allocated resources while awaiting assignment of others; and

No Preemption. No resource can be forcibly removed from a process holding it.

Clearly deadlock is an undesirable situation since if it is not dealt with properly the processes involved in the deadlock will wait forever, without furthering their execution. There are three main techniques for dealing with deadlock in an operating system:

Deadlock Prevention. Design the system in such a way that the possibility of deadlock is excluded. This can be accomplished by constraining resource requests to prevent one of the four conditions of deadlock. For example, the hold-and-wait condition can be prevented by requiring that a process request all of its resources at one time and blocking the process until all requests can be granted simultaneously.

Deadlock Avoidance. With this technique, a decision is made dynamically whether the current resource request will, if granted, potentially lead to a deadlock; if so, the request is denied. Deadlock avoidance thus requires knowledge of future process resource requests. A primary approach to deadlock avoidance utilizes the **Banker's algorithm**. The idea here is to determine if the current allocation of resources to processes represents a *safe state*: one in which there is at least one sequence of process resource requests that does not result in a deadlock; i.e. all of the processes can be run to completion.

Deadlock Detection. Resource request are granted to processes whenever possible. Periodically, the operating system executes an algorithm that checks if deadlock (circular wait) exists. If so, a *recovery strategy* is undertaken, namely one of the following.

  ◇ Abort all processes.

  ◇ Back up each deadlocked process to some previously defined checkpoint and restart all processes.

  ◇ Successively abort deadlocked processes until deadlock no longer exists.

  ◇ Successively preempt resources until deadlock no longer exists.

9.3 Overview of Resource Management in $\mathcal{OSP}$ 2

$\mathcal{OSP}$ 2 provides simulation support for deadlock avoidance and deadlock detection. This means that it understands the semantics of each of these two types of deadlock handling and provides appropriate error-checking facilities. For instance, in deadlock avoidance, a deadlock created after granting a resource allocation request to a process is considered an error, while in deadlock detection it is not.

The class `ResourceCB` does the bulk of the work. It represents the **resource control block**, where much of the information about the available resources is maintained. Resources are divided into **resource types**, where each resource type can have several **resource instances**. Each resource type is represented by a distinct resource control block.

A thread might issue a request to **acquire** a given number of instances of a particular resource type, but it does not care which particular resource instances are given to it as long as the instances are of the requested type. When such a request arrives, the operating system (which is part of the student code in class `ResourceCB`) must decide whether to grant the request, abort (kill) the requesting thread, or block the thread until its request is granted at some future time. This decision depends on the current state of resource allocation and on the deadlock-handling method (detection or avoidance) in use.

The class `RRB` represents **resource request blocks**. An RRB contains information about one outstanding request for one particular resource type issued by a particular thread. An `RRB` object is also an `Event` object (Section 1.6). When a thread issues a request that cannot be granted, the thread is suspended on the RRB associated with this request. Subsequently, when the needed resources become available, a `notifyThreads()` operation issued on that RRB will eventually wake up the thread.

The **resource table** is represented by the class `ResourceTable`; it is represented as an array of `ResourceCB` objects and lists all resource types available in the system. In $\mathcal{OSP}$ 2, all resource types are created at the beginning of simulation and no new resources are added or deleted afterwards. The total number of instances of each resource type remains constant as well. However, the number of *available* resource instances changes as processes acquire and release them.

Resource types are identified by a resource ID, a number between 0 and the resource table size, which is determined using the static method `getSize()` of class `ResourceTable`.

We will now describe the classes of package RESOURCES in detail. Figure 9.1

depicts the relationship these classes have with the other classes in the *OSP 2* system.

9.4 Class ResourceTable

This class is the simplest of them all: only a constructor is required. You can add other methods and variables to support your implementation of the project, but these would be specific to your particular design.

◇ public ResourceTable()
  Calls super() and might do additional initialization, if the student implementation defines additional fields in this class.

  OSP 2 provides the following built-ins that you will use to implement other classes in this project:

◇ public static final ResourceCB getResourceCB(int resourceID)
  Since resource types are identified using their numeric IDs, this method lets you visit, in a loop, the resource control block of every resource type in the system.

◇ public static final void getSize(int size)
  Returns the size of the resource table, which is also the number of resource types available in the system.

  Built-ins and relevant methods defined in other classes.   Since this class has only its constructor, your implementation will not use any methods provided by other *OSP 2* classes.

Summary of Class ResourceTable

This class is intended to maintain the resource table of the system. A resource table is simply a fixed-size array of resource objects. This size can be queried using the method getSize(). In addition, resource objects can be retrieved from the table using the getResourceCB() method, as described earlier.

Resources

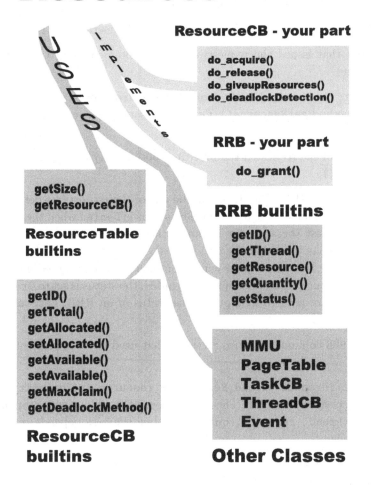

Figure 9.1   A diagram summarizing the package RESOURCES.

9.5 Class RRB

This class represents the resource request block, which threads use to specify their requests to the system. It is declared as follows:

◇ `public class RRB extends IflRRB`

Note that IflRRB extends class Event, which makes it possible to treat RRB objects as events. In particular, threads can be suspended on an RRB object and later resumed.

An RRB object includes the following information:

◇ The *ID*, which can be obtained with the help of the method getID().

◇ The *thread* that issued the request; it can be obtained using the method getThread().

◇ The *resource type* involved in the request. Its control block can be obtained using the method getResource(). Only one resource type can be requested using an RRB.

◇ The *quantity* of the requested resource. It is obtained by calling the method getQuantity().

◇ The *status* of the RRB. The status can be one of these constants defined by *OSP 2*: Denied, Suspended, Granted. The status is Denied when the system denies the request (because, for instance, the thread wants more resource instances than the total that the system has); it is Suspended if the system decides that the resource request cannot or should not be granted now, but can be in the future; when the request is granted, the status is set to Granted. Two methods are used to manipulate the status of an RRB: getStatus() and setStatus().

The class RRB contains only two methods that need to be implemented by the student:

◇ public RRB(ThreadCB thread,ResourceCB resource,int quantity)
This is the class constructor. The first statement in this constructor must be super(thread, resource, quantity), but the rest depends on your program design.

◇ public void do_grant()
This method is used to grant the RRB on which it is invoked. Note that do_grant() does not make any *decision* on whether to grant or not. This decision is made elsewhere, as described later in this chapter. Thus, this method does bookkeeping only. In particular, it decrements the number of available instances of the requested resource by the requested quantity and increments the number of allocated instances of this resource by that same quantity. The current number of available instances of a resource is given by the method getAvailable() and is set by the method setAvailable(). Similarly, the number of allocated resources is obtained and changed using the methods getAllocated() and setAllocated(), respectively.

To finish granting the request, the status of the RRB must be set to `Granted`
and the thread that was waiting on this RRB should be resumed. The latter
is done by invoking the method `notifyThreads()` of class `Event` (recall that
a RRB is also an `Event` object).

Built-ins and relevant methods defined in other classes.   The implementation of the methods in the RRB class relies on the following methods
provided by other classes (or inherited from the superclasses of RRB):

⋄ `final public int getStatus()`   RRB
   Returns the status of the RRB: `Denied`, `Suspended`, or `Granted`.

⋄ `final public void setStatus(int value)`   RRB
   Sets the status of the RRB to `Denied`, `Suspended`, or `Granted`.

⋄ `final public int getID()`   RRB
   Returns the ID of the RRB.

⋄ `final public int getQuantity()`   RRB
   Returns the quantity of the resource requested by the thread that issued
   the request.

⋄ `final public ThreadCB getThread()`   RRB
   The thread that issued the request.

⋄ `final public ResourceCB getResource()`   RRB
   The resource for which the request was issued.

⋄ `public final int getAvailable()`   ResourceCB
   Returns the number of free instances of this resource type.

⋄ `public final void setAvailable(int value)`   ResourceCB
   Sets the number of free instances of this resource type.

⋄ `public final int getAllocated(ThreadCB thread)`   ResourceCB
   Returns the number of allocated instances of this resource type.

⋄ `public final void setAllocated(ThreadCB thread,int value)`
                                                                   ResourceCB
   Sets the number of allocated instances of this resource type.

Summary of Class RRB

The class RRB is intended to maintain the information about requests that were
issued by the various threads for the non-shareable resources that are provided

by the system. As mentioned earlier, an RRB object has the following attributes:
ID, *thread*, *resource type*, the *quantity* of the requested resource type, and the
status of the request. These attributes can be queried and manipulated using
the methods described earlier in the section.

9.6 Class ResourceCB

This class does most of the work. In particular, this is where the deadlock
detection and avoidance algorithms are implemented. The deadlock-avoidance
algorithm is invoked by the do_acquire() method, while deadlock detection
is the responsibility of the method deadlockDetection(), which is invoked
periodically by $\mathcal{OSP}$ 2. The ResourceCB class is declared as follows:

◇ public class ResourceCB extends IflResourceCB

Most textbooks describe deadlock avoidance and detection algorithms in
terms of the various resource allocation and resource request matrices, which
are used for keeping track of the current state of system resources. This all looks
simple enough, except for one important point: textbook algorithms all assume
that all the threads and resource types are known in advance, so they represent
the matrices as two-dimensional arrays. In a real system, neither resources, nor
threads are static: they come and go and their total number cannot be assumed
to be bounded by a known constant. Therefore, matrices used by the *real-life*
deadlock-handling algorithms cannot be represented as two-dimensional arrays.

In $\mathcal{OSP}$ 2, the number of resource types is fixed, which simplifies things a
bit. However, the number of threads that can potentially request resources is
not known and cannot be estimated. Thus, using two-dimensional arrays for
representing resource allocation and request matrices is also out of the question:
you must come up with another suitable data structure. Since most operations
in deadlock-detection and -avoidance algorithms reference the matrix elements
via a specific resource and/or thread, your data structure must provide efficient
access to the matrix elements using either of these keys. For instance, if you
have to scan arrays and compare their entries to a particular thread ID or
resource, it is a sure sign that you have chosen a bad data structure.

One good data structure in this case would be an array of hash tables,
where each hash table represents all requests made by the various threads for
a particular resource type. Since Java hash tables are dynamic, they provide
exactly what the doctor ordered for this particular problem.

◇ public ResourceCB(int qty)

   This is the required class constructor. It must have super(qty) as its first statement, but the rest depends on your program design.

◇ public static void init()

As in other student modules, this method is called by the simulator at the beginning of simulation. It can be used to initialize the static variables and structures that you might use in your implementation.

◇ public RRB do_acquire(int quantity)

This method is typically invoked by an $\mathcal{OSP}$ 2 thread on a given resource type (represented by a ResourceCB object) in order to obtain quantity instances of that resource type. To determine which $\mathcal{OSP}$ 2 thread has issued the request, the following method can be used. First, the current task can be found from the *page table base register*, or PTBR; see Section 5.2 for more information on this subject. The value of the PTBR is the page table of the currently running task. In $\mathcal{OSP}$ 2, the value of the PTBR is obtained using the static method getPTBR() of class MMU, and the current task can be obtained from a page table via the method getTask().

Next, you have to create an RRB that describes the request. What follows depends on whether the simulator is in deadlock-avoidance or deadlock-detection mode (which is determined by an input simulation parameter that you might have spotted in the GUI window). To find out which mode is in effect, use the method getDeadlockMethod().

If the deadlock-handling method is Detection, there are three possibilities. If the system has enough available instances of the requested resource, the request is granted immediately by executing the method grant() on the RRB. If the requested number of instances cannot be granted under *any* circumstances (e.g., because the total number of instances of the requested resource type that are either held or requested by the given thread exceeds what the system has), then null is returned. If the requested number of instances cannot be granted immediately (but might be in the future, if all other threads release their resources) then the requesting thread must be suspended on the RRB and the RRB's status should be set to Suspended. The RRB status is set using the method setStatus(), while threads are suspended using the suspend() method of class ThreadCB. Recall that an RRB is an Event object as well, so in order to suspend a thread on an RRB, the RRB must be passed as a parameter to suspend(). Read more about thread suspension and resumption in Section 4.3.

If the deadlock-handling method is Avoidance, then you must use a deadlock-avoidance algorithm, such as the Banker's algorithm. If this algorithm says that it is safe to grant the request, the RRB is granted. Otherwise, the thread is suspended and the RRB status is set to Suspended as well.

When a thread is suspended inside do_acquire(), its execution is paused until the request is granted (possibly as a result of a release() operation on the same resource or of giveupResources() operation, which is invoked when a thread is killed), and the thread is resumed. Whether the RRB is granted immediately or the thread is suspended, do_acquire() returns the RRB that was created earlier in order to represent the request.

◇ public void do_release(int quantity)
This method might be invoked by an $\mathcal{OSP}$ 2 thread on a given resource type (represented by a ResourceCB object) in order to release quantity instances of that resource type.

As with do_acquire(), you first must find the thread that issued the release() request. Then the state of the resource allocation should be updated appropriately in order to reflect the new number of free resources and the new allocation of the given resource to the thread. Note that the thread might release some, but not all, instances held for this resource type. The exact details depend on your representation of the resource-allocation state, but this would typically involve the methods setAllocated(), setAvailable(), getAvailable(), etc.

This is not all, however. Since new resources became available after the release operation, it is possible that some of the previously suspended requests can now be granted. In order to be able to determine whether this is the case, one needs to keep track of the RRBs that were previously suspended in do_acquire(). Once a grantable RRB is found, it should be granted (using the grant() method) and the thread waiting on that RRB is resumed (resumption is done by method grant()).

◇ public static Vector do_deadlockDetection()
If the simulation method is Detection, this method will be periodically called by $\mathcal{OSP}$ 2 in order to test your implementation of the deadlock-detection algorithm. This method should first check if a deadlock exists and, if so, remove it. Your instructor might have imposed specific requirements on your implementation of deadlock detection and recovery, and $\mathcal{OSP}$ 2 adds its own.

First, there should be no deadlocks left after do_deadlockDetection() returns. The result returned by this method should be a vector of ThreadCB objects that were found to be involved in a deadlock. $\mathcal{OSP}$ 2 will compare this list with its own and will issue an error if the two lists differ. If no deadlock exists, null should be returned.

You can use any textbook deadlock-detection algorithm that can detect deadlocks in the presence of multiple instances per resource type. (For instance, cycle detection in a wait-for graph would *not* be a suitable algorithm for this purpose.)

Deadlock recovery is done by killing some or all of the threads involved in the deadlock. However, $\mathcal{OSP}\,2$ insists that threads must not be killed unnecessarily. This means that no thread should be killed unless it is deadlocked and, in addition, if the deadlock is gone after killing of *some* deadlocked threads, then no further thread destruction should occur.[1]

Threads are killed using the kill() method of class **ThreadCB**. Note that when a thread is killed, it releases its resources by calling do_giveupResources() (described next). As in the case of the do_release() method, this creates an opportunity for granting a previously suspended RRB and resuming the associated thread. See the description of do_release() to learn how to do this.

◇ public static void do_giveupResources(ThreadCB thread)

This method is called in order to release all resources previously allocated to **thread**, and it happens when **thread** is terminated. You will never need to call this method in this project. Instead, your implementation of this method is made available to *other* $\mathcal{OSP}\,2$ modules, which will call do_giveupResources() when necessary. This method should go over the resources allocated to the given thread and update the number of the available instances of such resources accordingly. The number of resources allocated to the thread should also be adjusted (to 0).

Since the thread releases its resources, the system might have enough free resources to unblock some suspended RRBs. Therefore, as in the case of do_release(), it is necessary to check the suspended RRBs and grant those that are grantable.

Built-ins and relevant methods defined in other classes. The following methods and fields, which are defined in other classes or are provided by the superclasses of **ResourceCB**, might be used in the implementation of the class **ResourceCB**.

◇ public final int getID()   ResourceCB
Returns the ID of the resource.

◇ public final int getTotal()   ResourceCB
Returns the total number of instances (free plus allocated) for this resource type.

---

[1] Note that if N threads are involved in the deadlock, then killing any $N-1$ of them will eliminate the deadlock. But often the deadlock can be eliminated by killing fewer than $N-1$ threads.

⋄ **public final int getAllocated(ThreadCB thread)**   ResourceCB
Returns the number of allocated instances of this resource type.

⋄ **public final void setAllocated(ThreadCB thread,int value)**
                                                              ResourceCB
Sets the number of allocated instances for this resource type.

⋄ **public final int getAvailable()**   ResourceCB
Returns the number of free instances of this resource type.

⋄ **public final void setAvailable(int value)**   ResourceCB
Sets the number of free instances for this resource type.

⋄ **public final int getMaxClaim(ThreadCB thread)**   ResourceCB
Returns the maximal number of instances of this resource type that can
ever be acquired by the given thread. Used for deadlock avoidance only.

⋄ **public final static int getDeadlockMethod()**   ResourceCB
Returns the deadlock-handling method currently in effect: Avoidance or
Detection.

⋄ **public final static int getSize()**   ResourceTable
Returns the size of the resource table. This value is also equal to the number
of different resource types in *OSP 2*.

⋄ **public static final ResourceCB getResourceCB(int resourceID)**
Given an index into the resource table, returns the ResourceCB object in
that table cell. This method makes it possible to visit the resource control
block of each resource type in a loop.

⋄ **static public PageTable getPTBR()**   MMU
Returns the value of the page table base register, which is either null or
the page table of the currently running task.

⋄ **public final TaskCB getTask()**   PageTable
Indicates which task owns the given page table. In RESOURCES, this method
is used to determine the thread that issued the request.

⋄ **public ThreadCB getCurrentThread()**   TaskCB
Returns the running thread of the currently running task.

⋄ **public RRB(ThreadCB thread, ResourceCB resource, int quantity)**
                                                              RRB
A constructor for creating resource request blocks with the given parameters.

⋄ **public final void grant()**   RRB
Grants the request represented by this RRB.

⋄ **final public void setStatus(int value)**   RRB
Sets the status of the RRB to Denied, Suspended, or Granted.

⋄ `final public ThreadCB getThread()`   RRB
The thread that issued the request represented by this RRB.

⋄ `final public ResourceCB getResource()`   RRB
The resource for which the request was issued.

⋄ `final public int getQuantity()`   RRB
Returns the quantity of the resource requested by the thread that issued
the request.

⋄ `final public void suspend(Event event)`   ThreadCB
Suspends the thread on which this method is called and puts the thread on
the waiting queue of `event`.

⋄ `final public void kill()`   ThreadCB
Kills this thread. Note that this will cause the thread to release its resources,
which in turn might make some previously suspended RRBs grantable.

⋄ `final public int getStatus()`   ThreadCB
Returns the status of the thread. See Section 4.3 for more information on
the different states of a thread. In this project you might need to know
that killed threads have status `ThreadKill`. If such a thread shows up in
a resource-allocation matrix or elsewhere, you might want to delete or skip
it in your algorithms.

⋄ `public void notifyThreads()`   Event
Resumes all threads that might be waiting on this event. In the case of
package RESOURCES, the event would be an RRB and the single resumed
thread would be the thread that issued the corresponding request.

Summary of Class `ResourceCB`

Instances of this class are used to represent individual non-shareable resources
in the system. An individual resource has the following attributes:

ID: The identity of the resource. This parameter can be retrieved using the
built-in `getID()`.

Total number of instances: This attribute describes the total number of instances of the resource that exist in the system. It can be obtained using
the built-in method `getTotal()`.

Number of allocated instances: The number of instances of the resource that
are currently allocated to a given thread. This parameter can be retrieved using the method `getAllocated()` and changed using the method
`setAllocated()`.

Number of free instances: This parameter represents the number of free instances of the resource. It can be obtained by calling the built-in method `getAvailable()` and changed using the method `setAvailable()`.

Maximum number of claimable instances: This parameter represents the maximal number of instances of a resource that can possibly be acquired by a single thread.

9.7 Methods Exported by the RESOURCES Package

Only one method defined in this package is used by other modules:

⋄ `public static void giveupResources(ThreadCB thread)` `ResourceCB`
Called by terminating threads in order to release the abstract shared resources held by that thread.

Index